Following the Yellow Arrow

Younger Pilgrims on the Camino

EDITED BY

Lynn K. Talbot

and

Andrew Talbot Squires

WingSpanPress

Printed in the United States of America
Published by WingSpan Press, Livermore, CA
www.wingspanpress.com
The WingSpan name, logo and colophon
are the trademarks of WingSpan Publishing.

First Edition 2011

Frontispiece drawing of scallop shell: Will Stauffer-Norris

Cover Photo: Lynn K. Talbot

Publisher's Cataloging-in-Publication Data
Talbot, Lynn K.
Following the yellow arrow : younger pilgrims on the Camino /
edited by Lynn K. Talbot and Andrew Talbot Squires.
p. cm.
ISBN: 978-1-59594-435-1 (pbk.)
ISBN: 978-1-59594-402-3 (hardcover)
ISBN: 978-1-59594-749-9 (ebk.)
1. Christian pilgrims and pilgrimages—Spain—Santiago de
Compostela. 2. Santiago de Compostela (Spain)—Description and
travel.   I. Squires, Andrew Talbot. II. Title.
BX2321.S3 T35 2011
263`.0424611—dc22
                                        2011921059

10 9 8 7 6 5 4 3 2 1

For Mike, husband and father

TABLE OF CONTENTS

INTRODUCTION

We were an unusual sight: a mother and son hiking the Camino de Santiago, first in 2004, then again in 2006. We covered hundreds of kilometers. We saw fathers and sons, mothers and daughters, fathers and daughters, but where were the mothers and sons? We never saw them. Similarly, when we looked at the books that had been published on the Camino, we found none that featured younger voices, none that recorded the fascination that many young people feel when they cross the Pyrennes, descend onto the long central Meseta, and finally arrive in Santiago. We wondered why.

Why does the Camino de Santiago attract so many pilgrims today? It's a recent phenomenon. In 1974, the routes were not marked, the *albergues* were nonexistent, and many sites along the way were not open. In 1986, fewer than 2,500 pilgrims arrived in Santiago; numbers did not surge until the 1990s. Yet the Camino has existed for more than a thousand years.

HISTORY

The Camino de Santiago, the medieval pilgrimage route that stretches westward across northern Spain from the Pyrenees to the Atlantic Ocean, was a major pilgrimage routes during the Middle Ages. Santiago de Compostela, along with Jerusalem and Rome, drew multitudes of pilgrims for its historical significance to Christendom. Why was pilgrimage so popular? Passionate religious beliefs, the desire to touch relics associated with a saint, the quest for a miracle — all spurred individuals toward pilgrimage. Through relics, a medieval pilgrim could appeal to a saint, who became an advocate for the individual in heaven. Many sites in Europe — e.g. Rocamadour, Conques, and Poitier — could claim fame based on fragmentary relics such as a piece of the Cross, a thorn from Christ's Crown, or a bone or piece of hair from a martyr. Monasteries and cathedrals sought relics that could attract pilgrims and so bring honor, fame, and money to their churches.

That isn't all. Pilgrimage could also serve as penance, imposed by a priest after confession, and even by judges for serious crimes. Penance offered pilgrims a chance of avoiding Hell. A journey might also be undertaken to present a petition — for a miraculous cure from illness, for the birth of a child, or for a renewal of faith. Others might go on pilgrimage to honor a vow made for the restoration of health or a victory in battle. And while most went on pilgrimage for religious reasons, some went simply to escape the drudgery of daily life, to escape the strict control of feudal lords, or simply to see another part of the world, a sort of medieval tourism.

Pilgrims could choose both their destination and their route, since pilgrimage sites arose throughout Europe and beyond. The link of Jerusalem and Rome to established Christianity made these destinations popular; the pilgrim to Jerusalem could follow the footsteps of Christ while Rome offered the Papacy. By contrast, in Santiago de Compostela, the pilgrim could visit the tomb of St. James, one of the Twelve Apostles. According to Christian tradition, James had preached on the Iberian Peninsula and then, when he returned to the Holy Land, had become the first martyred apostle. After his death, his body was miraculously transported to northwestern Spain, where he was buried. William Melczer in *The Pilgrim's Guide to Santiago de Compostela* (1993) traces the way ecclesiastical documents from the sixth or seventh century expanded the role of St. James in Spain, describing his travels on the peninsula and his burial in Spain. In the early ninth century, his tomb was "rediscovered" and the pilgrimage to Santiago began. Alfonso II (792-842), then king, was among the first to visit. He proclaimed Santiago the patron saint of Spain and erected a small chapel on the burial site.

The tomb's significance appears most clearly in the context of the historical reality of the Iberian Peninsula. Only the northern fringes were in Christian hands after Islamic forces had invaded in 711. These small Christian kingdoms began the *Reconquista*, as their attempt to reclaim the peninsula was called. As Christian troops gained strength and pushed south, they were aided by French nobles. Advantageous marriages between the ruling houses of Spain and France increased French influence in Spain's northern kingdoms — politically, economically, and ecclesiastically — and led eventually to the preeminence of the pilgrimage to Santiago. Proof lies in the scallop shell (even today symbolic of a pilgrim's journey to Santiago) which has been found in medieval tombs and churches throughout Europe.

The Benedictine order of Cluny, newly established along the Camino, secured prominence on the Iberian Peninsula and helped impose the Roman rite over the traditional Hispano-Visigothic rite, strengthening links with the rest of Europe. In the 12th century, Diego Gelmírez, the archbishop of Santiago, in order to expand the importance of Santiago and the pilgrimage route, transformed the modest church into one of the foremost Romanesque cathedrals in Europe. The Cluniac order also helped develop the route, building monasteries that could shelter pilgrims. Pope Calixtus II further expanded the importance of the route by establishing the privileges associated with the Compostelan Holy Years, when July 25 falls on a Sunday. The *Codex Calixtinus*, a 12th-century manuscript named in honor of this pope, includes miracles associated with Santiago, sermons and church music, a history that links Charlemagne to the pilgrimage, and provides the first travel guide to the Camino. The *Codex* details the dangers of the route, the quality of the food and water, and the types of people a pilgrim might encounter. Some regions are "full of evil and vicious people" (Melczer 76).

Pilgrim traffic rose dramatically. The sheer number of pilgrims — many thousands annually in the 11th and 12th centuries — required goods and services from those who lived along the Camino. Even town structures transitioned from a circular shape for protection, to an elongated form stretched out along the main road to maximize contact with pilgrims. Repopulation of northern Spain, necessary as Christian forces advanced toward the south, involved pilgrims who chose not to return to their own countries, spawning neighborhoods and whole towns inhabited by *"francos"* or foreign pilgrims, memorialized by street names such as Rúa de los Francos and by towns such as Villafranca del Bierzo.

After the 14th century, pilgrimage began to wane, due in part to spiritual abuses, such as the sale of indulgences which exposed Church greed, in part to new ideas from scientific discoveries, and in part to the Protestant Reformation. In 1520, Martin Luther declared, "All pilgrimages should be stopped. There is no good in them: no commandment enjoins them, no obedience attaches to them" (*To the Christian Nobility of the German Nation*). While Catholics continued to visit traditional shrines, the great age of European pilgrimage came to an end by the 16th century.

THE CAMINO TODAY

In the 20th century, the revitalization of the Camino de Santiago was a slow process which began after World War II. In the 1940s, academic studies in both Spain and France reawakened general interest in the pilgrimage route. But it was Galician priest Elias Valiña Sampedro, who brought today's Camino to life, writing in 1971 a compact guidebook for walkers, and in 1982, marking the Camino Francés with the beloved yellow arrows. Local pilgrimage associations and governmental agencies have carried on his work in marking the pilgrimage routes. In 1987, the Council of Europe designated the Camino de Santiago the first European Cultural Itinerary, and in 1993, UNESCO declared the Camino Francés a World Heritage Site. From just under 2,500 pilgrims arriving in Santiago in 1986, the number has risen exponentially, spiking in the Holy Years of 1993 (99,000), 1999 (155,000), 2004 (180,000), and 2010 (272,000). Many modern pilgrims have covered only the 100-kilometer minimum distance required for the pilgrim certificate, the *Compostela*, but many others have walked the 750 kilometers from the Spanish-French border. A few, like medieval pilgrims, have departed from their own homes. The rapid growth of the modern Camino has once again aided the economic health of the region. Pilgrims require shelter, restaurants, and shops.

But the large number of pilgrims threatens the camaraderie and the meaningful experiences that have long characterized the Camino. This issue remains unresolved.

Many thoughtful books have been written on the Camino (listed in "Further Reading"), but almost all reflect the experiences of older pilgrims. This volume presents another voice, that of younger pilgrims — those who walked the Camino in their teens and early twenties. What inspires these young people to walk? What do they learn about themselves? What enduring lessons do they bring home from their experience? A number of the contributors walked as part of college groups, since the Camino offers an ideal setting to learn about history, architecture, literature, and medieval studies. Some contributors walked alone, some with family members or friends. Some have walked more than once. Like medieval pilgrims, their modern counterparts have the same needs of shelter and food; the same concerns with heat, cold, rain, and difficult terrain; the same opportunities for reflection. On the Camino, a pilgrim becomes isolated from the distractions and stresses of daily life and enters a unique transformative space, which these twenty-one authors describe. They offer insights into why they walked, what they learned, and why the Camino can be a catalyst for change in their lives.

TWO HIKERS

We were a lonely sight: a mother and son hiking alone, along an empty stretch of the Camino, toward Santiago, the cold winds whipping our jackets, snow flying in our faces, our backpacks heavy. We say almost nothing. Instead, we experience the Camino as if a thousand years had been stripped away and we'd vanished into medieval history, connecting our lives to the landscape and spiritual presence that others, long before us, had experienced. We come to a bar, greet the owner, enjoy a *café con leche*, and continue on our way. That — the unique connection with people, landscape, and history — is the essence of the Camino. The essays that follow — though with a different resonance in their voices — also see the Camino uniquely: as a revelation, as a community of fellow pilgrims, as a spiritual awakening, as a lens into themselves, as an anchor for the lives they will shape. Whatever their experiences, these twenty-one writers discover that the Camino has helped configure who they are and what they wish to become. They link the past and the present.

In the Holy Year of 2010, we — Lynn and Andrew — celebrated its arrival in January by hiking the Camino once again. This time, as we walked, we thought about the enduring testament that a book of fresh essays, including the Afterword by Andrew, might offer readers familiar — and unfamiliar — with the Camino. It is in the spirit of hope and renewal that, in an era of great uncertainty, we offer these essays as avenues into personal transformation.

GLOSSARY OF SPANISH TERMS

The following terms have become part of the pilgrim vocabulary.

albergue — a pilgrim hostel which usually requires a *credencial* as proof of pilgrim status

bocadillo — a 6- to 8-inch long piece of crusty bread, sliced in half and filled with cheese, ham, sausage or potato omelet (*tortilla española*)

bordón — staff, walking stick

¡Buen Camino! — a typical greeting on the Camino, comparable to "Have a good trip!"

café con leche — expresso coffee with hot milk

caña — draft beer

caldo gallego — a traditional Galician soup made with white beans, greens, potatoes and pork

chorizo — pork sausage

compañero, compañera — companion, comrade

Compostela — the certificate issued by the Cathedral in Santiago to pilgrims who have walked the last 100 kilometers of the Camino (200 kilometers if traveling by bicycle or horse)

credencial — the "pilgrim passport," a booklet issued to pilgrims as proof of pilgrim status; the *credencial* is stamped in *albergues*, churches, cafés, and other establishments to verify the distance traveled (for the *Compostela*)

galletas — cookies

hórreo — a granary raised on stone pillars, found in northern Spain

hospitalero, hospitalera — the person in charge of an *albergue*, either a volunteer or paid

lomo — pork loin

magdalenas — small sponge cakes typically eaten for breakfast with *café con leche*

palloza — a typical circular or oval thatched hut of pre-Roman origin, found in Galicia and León

panadería — bread store

peregrino, peregrina — pilgrim

refugio — another term for an *albergue*

ultreia — a traditional pilgrim greeting roughly meaning "onward;" also the title of a traditional pilgrim's song

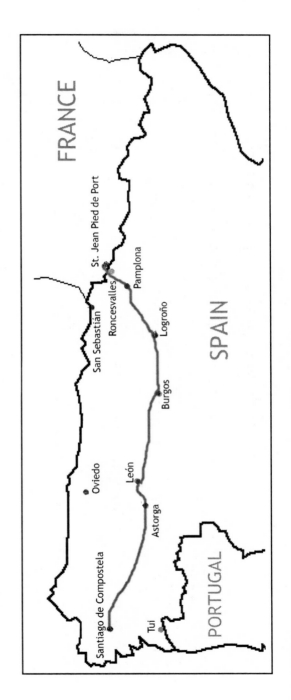

CAMINO FRANCÉS

ALTERNATE CAMINO ROUTES IN SPAIN

Camino del Norte—runs along the northern coast from San Sebastián

Camino Aragonés—crosses into Spain 45 miles east of Roncesvalles and joins the Camino Francés shortly after Pamplona

Camino Portugués—begins in Oporto and crosses into Spain at Tui

Camino Primitivo—begins in Oviedo and joins the Camino Francés shortly before Santiago

Camino del Salvador—connects León and Oviedo

BEFORE THE YELLOW ARROW

Lynn K. Talbot

May 25, 1974. The ancient train slowly chugged into the station at St. Jean Pied de Port. It had been a long journey. I had left Madrid the night before, crossed the border at Irún and had waited many hours in Bayonne for this train to depart. As I arrived in St. Jean, the doubts that had begun during my journey northward exploded. What was I doing here? What indeed was I thinking when I signed up for this trip?

Six months earlier, while studying in Madrid, I had seen an intriguing flyer inviting me to "Walk 500 miles on the Camino de Santiago!" It was an announcement for a two-month Medieval Studies seminar focused on the history, literature, art, and architecture of the Camino which would be taught as we walked from St. Jean to Santiago de Compostela. I was captivated by the opportunity — it was a chance to explore the small towns of northern Spain; more importantly, it would allow me to spend another two months in Spain — and it seemed like an unforgettable adventure! But now it was May and I had to face the reality of that decision — did I want to walk 500 miles? Could I? Soon I would find out.

So it began. Our group consisted of six other women (a mix of graduate and undergraduate students) and our professor, David Gitlitz, a medievalist from Indiana University. All of us were ready for a memorable experience, but we didn't know what challenges awaited us.

The Camino de Santiago in 1974 was very different from the Camino today. There was no marked path for pilgrims

3

on foot, no yellow arrows to follow, no pilgrim's *credencial* to validate our journey, no *albergues*, and no other pilgrims. While contemporary scholars had published studies on the historic past, the Camino now existed primarily as an automobile route. The Spanish Ministry of Tourism had the route well detailed in travel brochures and marked with roads signs at the entrance to important towns, indicating points of cultural significance and the remaining distance to Santiago. But that was all.

The eight of us set out to follow the historical French route, the best-known variant of the Camino and the one that pilgrims in centuries past had described in their published accounts. David carried Spanish Army topographical maps of the areas we would cross to aid him in selecting a route. But our actual route was determined by frequent conversations with locals: "Can we walk from Puente la Reina to Estella other than on the highway?" "What's the best way to get to Triacastela?" Often these people would point out a farming road or a footpath from one town to the next. Sometimes we would get lost — no yellow arrows to point the right direction — and perhaps a shepherd or a farmer would re-orient us or suggest a better route. But at times we were forced to walk along the highway — no chance of getting lost — but certainly far from the medieval experience that we were studying. In spite of the challenges of getting from one town to the next, our route was filled with intriguing surprises. We saw daily rural life in unexpected depth, from chatting with a shepherd holding a minutes-old lamb, to watching wheat being threshed by hand using traditional methods, to observing the harsh living conditions endured by rural farmers — memorable moments that have stayed with me since.

I remember the excitement of those first days of hiking — the unexpected newness of traveling on foot and its slowed pace, the spectacular scenery, the close-up view of rural life — all tempered by the realities of big blisters and sore feet. I had backpacked previously, but the daily demands of walking long distances and enduring heat, rain, thirst and exhaustion were more than I had expected. Even my equipment by today's high-tech standards was laughable: big, heavy, leather boots with little padding, jeans, cotton T-shirts, and a sweater for warmth. Eventually, though, the blisters healed and the excitement faded, and I grew accustomed to, even enjoyed, the pace allowed by foot travel.

My journal from that trip is filled with references to weather (heat, cold, rain), terrain (steep inclines, treacherous downhill slopes, the interminable flat Meseta), and trail conditions (muddy, dusty, rocky, slippery), much like the reactions of today's pilgrims. But we endured far harsher conditions — bushwhacking down the Alto de Perdón through thorny bushes because there was no trail, struggling across a rough plowed field or through shoulder-high wheat to rejoin a path we had missed, getting lost in the fog of the Montes de Oca, and often walking many extra kilometers because of our mistakes — all because the Camino as we know it today did not exist. Yet in our two-and-a-half months of walking, we experienced so much. We followed the annual rhythm of nature, watched the maturation of the wheat from short, bright green shoots to tall, golden yellow stalks turning into the stubble of harvest, enjoyed the wild profusion and the extraordinary variety of wildflowers — poppies, cornflowers, foxglove, and heather — and marveled at moments of great beauty, such as a heavy rain followed by the glittering iridescence of a rainbow.

There were no other pilgrims on the road, so we attracted lots of attention. Newspapers in Burgos and Santiago wrote articles about us, and we were interviewed on the radio in Burgos. When we would walk into a town, people stared at our group, which made me feel uncomfortable, but once we would speak to them, they were exceedingly courteous and friendly, especially in the small towns. They always had lots of questions: "Where are you from? What are you doing? Where are you staying?" People would come out of their houses to watch us pass, and sometimes they seemed to know that we were coming, because they had heard news of a group of pilgrims on the road. One old man in a small town on the Meseta — to win an argument that everything he heard on the radio was true — declared: "Yesterday I heard on the radio that there was a group of Americans in Burgos following the Camino de

Santiago, and today, here they are in our bar!" An old man in Cizur Menor, just outside of Pamplona, told us about other pilgrims whom he had seen: a group on horseback dressed in 15th-century dress three or four years before, and two French couples two years previous. So pilgrim traffic in the seventies was very light.

Older people always had time to talk to us. Elderly ladies dressed all in black would show us their vegetable gardens, and groups of older men, wearing their black berets and carrying canes, would talk about farming while basking in the attention of young foreign women. The children were the most excited to see us and, with their usual innocence, they would ask direct questions about anything that occurred to them. David wore the traditional medieval pilgrim's hat, a wide-brimmed grey felt creation with the front held up by a cockle shell. We saw lots of smiles and laughter, and children would ask: "Why does that man have a funny hat on?" We also met many young people our age and often they invited us to join their activities. We arrived in Castrogeriz for the fiesta of San Juan and in the afternoon, a crowd of young people invited us to a *chocolatera*. Someone had made a huge pot of hot chocolate, thick like pudding in the Spanish style, and we took it to an empty barn where we ate it using cookies to scoop up the chocolate. The next day, the same young people invited us again to their party at the old barn, where we sang, danced, and partied until the early morning hours.

We also attracted the attention of the Guardia Civil, the feared rural police force founded in the 19th century. In 1974 Spain was still a dictatorship, under the regime of Francisco Franco, and the Guardia Civil, which always patrolled in pairs, was responsible for maintaining control of the countryside. Frequently, we would stop in a small town's cafe for a drink or something to eat, and within a short period of time, two *guardias* in their three-cornered patent-leather hats would come in to see who we were and what we were doing there. They always were around when something unusual was happening. At first their presence intimidated us, but later it would make us smile because we knew why they had stopped in. There were other

6

indications of control in that conservative society: in the heat of the Meseta, we hiked in our shorts and when we arrived in Mansilla de las Mulas, we were greeted by a man who sang a little song about the mayor's recent edict, prohibiting women from walking around "half-naked." A few blocks later, a policeman told us to change into long pants because we were offending the morality of the town.

The lack of pilgrim *albergues* meant that we had to find our own lodgings, which led to some unforgettable experiences. Inexpensive hotels were always available, but we first sought more authentic pilgrim accommodations. Each day, one member would drive the group's van to the day's destination to secure lodging and food. David had written beforehand to the parish priests of the towns in which we would be spending the night and many times they suggested places where we could stay, or at times, had already arranged a place for our group. We slept in hay barns, in old school buildings, in unused municipal buildings, and in convents. Often there were no beds and we slept on the floor, and at times, no running water or bathrooms were available. I was always grateful just to have a place to sleep, but I complained in my journal about the lack of basic comforts. We enjoyed a respite from the primitive conditions when we stayed in *paradores*, the historical government-run hotels, in Santo Domingo de la Calzada, León, and Santiago de Compostela, all of which had served as pilgrim hospitals in medieval times (but where our pilgrim attire ran counter to the current upscale elegance of these hotels). The clean sheets, big fluffy towels, and unending hot water combined with the historical significance of the buildings made these stops special and helped us cope with the less comfortable conditions elsewhere.

The nights that I remember most, however, have nothing to do with comfort. Three nights are particularly memorable, because of our unique lodging and what these places taught me about Spanish hospitality and the realities of Spain at that time. In Nájera, we stayed at a convent of cloistered Franciscan nuns in the rooms reserved for visiting families. While there were not beds for everyone, our space was peaceful and clean.

The nuns at the convent asked if we would be willing to talk to them and of course we said yes. The visitation room was separated into two spaces by a double set of iron grates, about a foot apart, with the nuns' side covered by a curtain. In the late afternoon, the Mother Superior came to the grate and opened the curtain to see if we were ready. Then all the nuns — a total of 24, both young and old — came into their side and crowded as close as possible to their grate, some of them standing on chairs to see over the others' heads. All talked at once, asking questions about our trip, and at first, five different conversations were going on at once. They seemed so eager to know about our life as pilgrims and what we had experienced. They shared a little about their life in the convent and invited us to join their order. Having never spoken to a nun before, I was both intrigued and baffled by their words and by their decision to become nuns. It was a choice that I could not understand, but these women seemed at ease with their life. The next morning, we had promised the nuns that we would attend their Mass at which they sang hymns, including several set to American folk tunes, but with Spanish words. When we returned to our rooms, the nuns had set out breakfast for us — coffee, bread, preserved figs, and *chorizo*, all of which they had made. They came in for a tearful farewell and gave us religious cards while we were eating. They promised to pray for us while we walked, and we promised to say a prayer to Santiago for them when we arrived.

After hiking through the Montes de Oca, we arrived at the isolated church and monastery at San Juan de Ortega. The priest from the nearby town of Atapuerca, don José María Alonso Marroquín, allowed us to spend two nights in the monastery, which had recently been restored by the Spanish government. However, at that time, there was a legal dispute over ownership and use of the building and it therefore was unoccupied. The conditions were primitive: no beds, a bathroom without water, and a kitchen with only cold water, but the surroundings were authentic, as the monastery had received pilgrims over many centuries. Even our arrival there had evoked medieval times, for as we reached a high point, we could look down with relief at our day's destination, an isolated church and monastery even in the twentieth century. We ate dinner in Atapuerca, as there was nowhere to eat at the monastery. Afterwards, we talked to many of the locals, mostly men between 35 and 40. From the priest we learned there were few single women between the ages of 15 and 35 in any of the nearby towns, as they had left to find jobs and an easier life in the cities. Consequently, the men who stayed to work the land didn't marry and the priest predicted that within 20 years, no one would be left there working the land. He offered to marry any of us to these lonely bachelors. The next day, the priest took us to a nearby cave that had prehistoric cave paintings, although those accessible to us had been partially destroyed by graffiti. While even then, anthropologists were aware of the significance of the area, the major archeological finds that have brought fame to the area had yet to be discovered. The priest, don José María, later became the priest at the church at San Juan de Ortega and gained fame for the garlic soup he served to pilgrims following evening Mass.

Foncebadón was nearly abandoned when we stayed there, with only a few inhabitants who were planning to leave at summer's end. The only place to stay was a hay barn, built of rock with a straw roof and surrounded by four or five houses in ruins, which belonged to one of the few people left in town. Three-quarters of the buildings in Foncebadón were in the process of becoming rubble. The sense of isolation was strong, especially when cold fog began rolling in, blotting out even the nearby buildings. With no electricity available, we were forced to go to bed when the sun set. We then understood how life in these mountain towns was too difficult to sustain them when better jobs were available in the cities. We had walked through similar nearly abandoned towns all across northern Spain, but staying overnight in one of these towns was enlightening.

Finding a place to eat outside of cities could also be challenging. Meals could be unexpected combinations of foods, such as fried eggs and rice for dinner, or simply picnic-food for all three meals. At times, there wasn't enough food available in a village to prepare a meal for eight people. Then, since we had a van with us, we would purchase the ingredients for dinner in a larger town and find someone in a local bar willing to cook the food for us. Meals often were served Spanish-style, such as a large platter of salad served with forks and no plates. Anyone who ate with the group discovered that you had to eat fast, as we, hungry pilgrims, would quickly devour any food placed on the table. Yet what I most remember about eating is the camaraderie of sharing a common table with others and the give-and-take of conversation, the picnic lunches of crusty bread and cheese in flower-filled meadows, and quaint restaurants that served hearty, home-cooked food.

Our pilgrimage was also a unique academic experience as the route guided what we studied. We read the *Song of Roland* at Roncesvalles and the *Poem of the Cid* in Burgos. A medieval castle would be the site of a history lesson. We studied Romanesque architecture at Eunate and Frómista and Gothic architecture at the cathedrals in Burgos and León. Each student was responsible for an in-depth study of a specific town — its history, economy, art and architecture — and then served as our guide and teacher as we explored the town.

We met several of the well-known Camino figures on our trip. In St. Jean, we spent an afternoon at the home of Madame Debril, perhaps the most feared guardian of the Camino. It was she, who in the early days of the modern Camino, determined whether one was a true pilgrim or not, and she would deny the coveted pilgrim stamp if she decided one was not a true pilgrim. When we were there, she pulled out sheets of red felt and commanded us to cut out, from a pattern, a Cross of Santiago which we then glued onto our backpacks. And by chance, we met Walter Starkie, author of *The Road to Santiago: Pilgrims of St. James* (1957), a classic early study of the pilgrimage route, in the Museo de los Caminos in Astorga. By then an old man, he shared his thoughts on the medieval Camino and his own experiences on the route when working on his book. But perhaps the most memorable person we met was don Elías Valiña Sampedro, the parish priest in O Cebreiro. He had already written his doctoral dissertation in 1965 entitled *El Camino de Santiago. Estudio histórico-jurídico* and his first guidebook, published in 1971, entitled *Caminos a Compostela*. But he later gained fame as the originator of the yellow arrows, which he began painting in 1982 to guide pilgrims and so encourage a resurgence of the pilgrimage route. When we arrived at O Cebreiro (then El Cebreiro, as all place-names were required to be in Castillian Spanish), don Elías was already promoting pilgrimage by restoring buildings into a small hotel, a restaurant, and a hay barn for pilgrim accommodations, where we stayed. There was even a book in which pilgrims could record their reflections on their journey, an item commonly found in most pilgrim *albergues* today. I feel lucky to have met these three people, for their insights into the early Camino and their contributions to today's Camino have enriched my own experience on the Camino.

Our arrival in Santiago on 28 July was a moment of both overwhelming joy and sadness. Like pilgrims of old, we raced to see who would reach the Monte de Gozo first (David — he had longer legs), but from the crest of the hill, we could make out the towers of the cathedral through the heavy haze. We felt jubilant and almost speechless that, after walking five hundred miles, before us was our goal. At the entrance of the city, we found a Romanesque cross with an inscription on the base: *Peregrino — todos los caminos del mundo llegan a Compostela* [Pilgrim — all the roads of the world lead to Compostela] — a fitting description for what we had just lived over the past two-and-a- half months. Our first view of the front of the cathedral was full of tourists, so strange after the isolation of walking through small towns and the countryside. We entered the cathedral and completed the time-honored rituals: fitting our hand into the Tree of Jesse at the Pórtico de la Gloria, climbing the narrow staircase behind the main altar to hug the statue of St. James, and descending below the altar to see the silver box containing the saint's (alleged) remains. We received our *Compostela*, the certificate that verifies one's pilgrimage — David presented them to us after requesting them in the cathedral as there was no formalized procedure at that time for obtaining the *Compostela*. While we stayed a few more days in the city to explore the cathedral, visit museums, and wrap up

11

our course, our pilgrimage had ended and we were left with a feeling of hollowness, as if something were missing. It was then that I understood that what had mattered was not the final destination, but the road that we had walked.

Did the pilgrimage change me? It did, and not in ways that I had expected. While the search for adventure compelled me to begin my journey, while I learned more than I had ever expected about Spanish art, architecture, history, and medieval literature, while I gained a deeper appreciation for rural life in Spain, and while I met many wonderful, unforgettable people, I finished the pilgrimage with a deeper spiritual understanding of myself. Like many young people who were raised with Sunday School and weekly church services, once in college, I had drifted away from religious practice. My pilgrimage altered that attitude — I had not anticipated the extraordinary contemplative effect of walking the Camino. For those two-and-a-half months, I left behind the hectic pace of classes, work, and social activities. My life was reduced to a simple daily routine — to walk to the next stopping point. The rhythmic beat of footsteps, the natural surroundings, the direct connection between me and the earth helped clear my mind and led me to connect with a deeper inner voice and to focus on who I was, my values, my moral compass, and who I wanted to be. I felt a deep bond with the millions of pilgrims who had walked before me, as if I had become part of their road, seeking answers to life's deepest questions, sensing the splendor of cathedrals and tiny chapels, touching the same magnificent sculptures, and experiencing warm hospitality along the way. But it was my arrival in Santiago where all these sensations came together and where my entrance into the square in front of the cathedral illuminated the spiritual nature of my pilgrimage. Walking into the cathedral was one of the most memorable moments of my life, for I knew that I had entered God's house. It is a memory that stays with me even now.

I feel fortunate to have walked the Camino de Santiago when I did. I treasure experiencing it in an untouched state, when the Camino didn't exist except as an historical fact. To be able to see now how the route has again come alive as a functional route for modern-day seekers gives me pleasure. The symbiotic relationship between the needs of pilgrims and those willing to provide services has helped regenerate the route's economic health. Much as in medieval times, when the pilgrimage route contributed to the economic development of northern Spain, today's pilgrimage has brought alive towns, such as Grañón and Rabanal del Camino, that were on the verge of disappearing. And today's pilgrims, whose motivation for walking often differs from that of medieval times, may find that the road still has the capacity to change them and their view of the world.

FONCEBADÓN

Deborah Gitlitz

I wasn't going to make it.

In the wind and lashing rain the plastic poncho clung to my body like a lovesick manta ray. My boot slipped on a muddy rock and pain tightened my shin. Wrestling back my hood — it snapped straight back like a weather sock — I squinted up the mountainside, searching for the tiny figures ahead. Rain needled my face. How far behind had I fallen? A gust of rain whipped by and I caught a glimpse of stones heaped among low bushes — the remains of a house or just more mountain rocks? The uneven trail twisted up and away from me into the fog of rain. Somewhere up there my companions plodded on. Somewhere up there I hoped we'd find a shelter with intact walls. I hoped we'd find it soon. I rubbed my leg, willing it to carry me a little farther. Dragging my hood up again I plastered it back on my wet head to cut the wind and, gritting my teeth, I pushed slowly on.

The adventure had begun with such promise.

On a sunny day in Urdos, France, we had set off into the Pyrenees, boots still clean, scallop shells freshly sewn to our backpacks, amazed to be here at last. *Profe* David strode energetically up the trail in cut-off jeans and a broad-brimmed hat, *bordón* in hand. *Profe* Linda and we eight student pilgrims tramped merrily along in his wake among snowy peaks and across swathes of wildflowers. In the chilly mountain pass between countries we stopped to savor the moment, before

17

stepping over the border and down the mountain into Spain, into the twelfth century, into our summer as pilgrims.

The plan was this: Professors David and Linda would shepherd our band of eight American students across Spain along the historical pilgrim route, the Camino, to Santiago. We'd spend the summer studying medieval literature, history, architecture and art. We would speak only Spanish. We would sleep on the floors of monasteries and schools; attend mass in tiny Romanesque chapels; eat cheese and bread in the shade of cypress trees. And in between we'd walk and walk and walk nine hundred kilometers across northern Spain to St. James' cathedral in Santiago de Compostela.

Like the others, I was nervous, giddy, buzzing with excitement. I had worked hard to get here: studying Spanish; sweating over my application essays; acquiring my international driver's license; researching towns along the Camino. At seventeen, I was the youngest student by several years; but I had been waiting longer than anyone for this trip.

I had been waiting my whole life. *Profe* David is my father.

In 1974 Dad led his first audacious, experimental trek to Santiago. I grew up on the stories he and Linda brought back: the rivers forded; the priests and goatherds befriended; the floors they slept on in villages where pilgrims hadn't been sighted in hundreds of years. The romance, the time travel, the adventure of it all bewitched me and I dreamed of the day I'd earn my scallop shell and set my boots on the Road.

Now here I was on that Road at last. That first afternoon we'd descended from the Pyrenees and tromped into Canfranc, dusty and elated, in time — as part of our pilgrim immersion experience — to attend our first local mass, blending in not at all with the congregation of five rusty old women and one sleepy dog. And that first night I lay in the dark in the little room I shared with two *compañeras*, wiggling my tired toes under the rough coverlet, gazing with satisfaction at our clustered boots airing on the windowsill. Jubilant to be a *peregrina* at last.

As the blisters on our heels swelled, burst and thickened into callus, we grew comfortable in our pilgrim rhythm. Rising

18

early, we'd breakfast lightly on crackers, fruit and cheese, standing around some cold stone anteroom or bristly field in our half-laced boots. We'd set out walking in the brief cool of morning; break for a shady lunch in the mid-day's heat; and straggle into a new town mid-afternoon in time to hold classes. We walked on trails, paved roads, dirt tracks, and cobbled streets. Sometimes we set off cross-country following nothing more than a topographical map and the logic of the terrain. Along the way we'd explore the architecture of roadside chapels and map the history and literature we were studying to the landscape we traversed. I added useful new words to my vocabulary, like *ampolla* ("blister") and *arbotante* ("flying buttress"). I learned where to buy stamps (the tobacconist's), and to glance up at the village steeples to see the messy nests of clatter-beaked storks.

Every day a different student drove ahead with the duffel bags to arrange in brave, faltering Spanish the evening's lodging and a meal somewhere: in the restaurant, the bar, perhaps the kitchen of a local *señora*. The designated student figured out where to buy breakfast and where we could gather for class. She'd ask around to find the man with the key to the church or other buildings of note. Most towns were small, built of brick and stone. Cobbled streets wandered their mazy medieval paths around the little shady plazas, the churches, the shops selling bread and vegetables and cigarettes from shallow storefronts. Outer streets might be paved; bigger towns had their unpretty commercial outskirts. Once we fell in love with a giant sycamore tree in a town plaza and we all climbed up with our binders to hold class in its octopus embrace.

I spent my free time studying or exploring town with my fellow students. I had hoped to find a friend among the five other girls and the two guys, someone to laugh and trade stories with. But it turned out that I had little in common with the others. They were amiable enough, but our various inclinations toward earnestness or partying (them) or general curiosity and goofball jokes (me) never quite lined up. We got along fine, but I was disappointed, and a bit lonely. Dad and Linda, the professors, had classes to prepare and old acquaintances to call upon. They were careful to treat me like the others, and to give me room to forge my own pilgrimage experience. This made an odd, new reserve between us. I missed our easy banter. I missed being family. Still, I was absorbed with the fascinating culture shock of student pilgrim life.

It wasn't until the second week, on the hilly hike to Berdún, that I felt the first cramp in my leg.

I walked through the ache, grimacing, until it subsided; but the next morning it was back, sharper, alongside both shins. By the third morning the pain was so fierce that after a single kilometer I had to hobble to the side of the road, tears in my eyes, to wait for the day's driver to scoop me up. It happened again the next day. And the next day, and the one after that: within the morning's first kilometer crippling cramps would begin to drag at my shins. My muscles burned and seized; walking felt like pushing through scalding, quick-setting cement. Gritting my teeth I'd step, stumble, and drag to a stop. Then I'd sit on my pack by the side of the road, dusty and despondent, as my family and my companions vanished around a bend I'd never know. In an hour, sometimes two, the day's driver would cart me to the next town.

My pilgrimage was suddenly a tangle of fear, frustration, and heartbreak. The pain in my legs was sharp and terrifying. My body had never betrayed me before; I wondered how badly I'd hurt myself, and for how long, and how much damage more walking might do. I was desperate to walk. I am the hiker who loves to be in front. I like to set the pace; I crave the unspoiled view, the chance to watch the path unscroll before me. I hate to go home before I've found out what's around every corner. And here I was, maddeningly benched. Valley after valley, monastery after standing stone after river after adventure passed me by, somewhere out there on the glittering Camino; while I drove disconsolately along the ordinary roads between towns. My last *ampollas* healed. I spent my mornings writing in plazas or bartering for mandarins and olives, while my companions were out in the countryside scouting for Roman

20

pot shards and exploring roadside Romanesque chapels. It was torture.

We visited doctors, of course. We went to hospitals in two different towns. All said the same, sensible thing: Your legs cannot heal if you walk. You must not walk for at least six weeks.

In six weeks the pilgrimage would be nearly over. There would not be another for at least five years, and then it would be my sister's turn. This pilgrimage was mine, and the only one I'd get; and it was passing me by. Already we were leaving behind the lovely eastern hills for the hot plains of north-central Spain.

I laced up my boots. I gritted my teeth, hoping the damage wouldn't last. I sent up a plea to St. James.

I walked.

My luck began to turn as I found that the *llanura*, the plains, were kinder to my legs. The melting heat of July warmed my beleaguered muscles and I moved more easily over the flat terrain. In the mornings when my legs were slow I'd sometimes notice Linda dawdling nearby, pointing out flowers or the bronzy curve of a sunburnt field. Or I'd find Dad ambling beside me, eyes bright, speculating about the lay of the land and who might have lived on it. Once my legs limbered up the two of us would pick up speed, singing rounds and ballads to the beat of our boots pounding the red dirt. We'd spoken nothing but Spanish all summer, which shaped us into slightly different selves; but songs were somehow exempt from that iron custom, and in this Spanish landscape it was sweetly disorienting to harmonize with my father on the familiar songs from home.

Beginning our trek so far east, we had been almost alone on the road all these weeks. But now we began to encounter occasional other pilgrims: an athletic pair of German hikers; a French devotee en route to Saint Jacques; a bearded Spaniard hiking the breadth of the country *descalzo*, barefoot. For a few days we kept pace with a lively Catholic youth group from Madrid; they were always leaving a town just as we arrived, and they'd turn to holler greetings, all fifteen of them waving madly.

Small surprises abounded. Once while sitting on a plaza bench I met a pair of Belgian punks (through their effusive German shepherd, Lobo). One wore high-tops with neon-orange laces; the other had a mohawk and a hypodermic needle around his neck on a string. No scallop shells, but I was awed to learn they'd begun their pilgrimage in Belgium in March. If I understood correctly, they were walking the road as the alternative to a jail sentence. It didn't seem polite to ask for what.

Another afternoon in the wavering heat we refilled our canteens at a little town fountain. Suddenly a flood of sheep engulfed us, rushing first to the trickling fountain and then to the adjacent concrete laundry pool. They were so single-minded in their charge, pressing in to the pool, that the front-row sheep kept toppling, bug-eyed, into the water. I laughed so hard I spilled my canteen, but the *pastor* just eyed us mildly as if to say, "Well, they're sheep. What do you expect?"

June eased into July, the flat plains unrolled before us, and the muscles in my legs unkinked gratefully. After a few morning twinges they'd loosen up and set me free to tramp along in the dust on the road to plenary indulgence, sweaty and joyful among the endless wheat fields and bright dancing poppies. One morning as we followed an orange dirt road paved with flattened sheep droppings my eye somehow picked out one bronzy circle among the millions and I stopped to look. When I picked it up I found in my palm a weathered coin embossed with a castle on one side and a fanciful lion on the other: a 17th-century relic of the united kingdoms of Castilla y León — history underfoot, and myself a part of the long tradition of this road. I was happy.

But in mid-July the smooth land rumpled up into hills once again and the damaged muscles in my legs revolted. The hot mornings found me sweating in pain, forcing my legs through their private cement, trudging along the road in a haze of distraction and willpower. On the downhills I was all right, but the *subidas*, the climbs, especially early in the day, defeated me. I cursed the medieval farmers for tucking their villages into the fertile valleys, forcing me to start my days by climbing painfully up and out. Slowly I'd fall to the end of the line, my view of the road smudged with angry tears and cluttered up with all those dusty, unfettered legs bounding along ahead of me. Often on those mornings *Profe* David, happily talking history at the front of the pack, would stop to tie his boot or casually linger, considering the map, until he wound up walking at my side. If the pain was really bad he'd sit with me and rub my calves; mostly he'd walk along with me companionably, chatting. Or he'd distract me with new songs to learn: English ballads full of coal miners and messy love affairs; Peruvian laments and tongue-twisting Spanish drinking songs. Despite the pain there was a sweetness to these mornings. I would have traded my Castilla y León coin for a pain-free, carefree pilgrimage, no question. But the path I was on had its own roadside surprises, and this was one: this new kind of friendship, pilgrim-daughter with pilgrim-dad.

This particular morning, though, had started out fine. My legs weren't bad and the usually blazing sun was tucked well behind clouds as we left Astorga early, setting out for the mountain village of Foncebadón. Given what we'd heard, our best hope for lodging was to find an empty building with its roof intact. The last time Dad and Linda stayed in the village, eight years before, its sole inhabitants were one old woman, her shambling son, and a handful of sheep. The place was now indicated on the map as *"Foncebadón (abandonado)."*

Not long into the morning a thin rain began, and it proved tenacious. But the rocky, undulating countryside, thatched with wild thyme and lavender, made a lovely change from the tedious wheat fields. Stone fences wandered across the hills, and among the straw-roofed stone houses, the rock rose was in bud. Here and there was a pine, the first trees we'd glimpsed in weeks.

All morning the rain streamed lightly down. The mountain we were to climb in the afternoon drew closer. The plan was to lunch in the town of Rabanal, but rumors of Roman mines lured us off the road into an adjacent valley. The rain got rainier and the wind got windier. It began to grow cold. We found the unimpressive remains of the mines: a shallow ditch (once a canal) and a ridge of thorn-covered dirt. The track indicated on our map dissolved into a mire on the wrong side of a tall ridge. We slogged along, heads down to keep the rain out of our eyes, ponchos over backpacks, a straggly line of hump-backed, mud-colored trudging tents. The rain and the wind picked up some more. My legs started to ache as we battled our way over the ridge through a tangled, trackless field that had been charred completely black. Brambles grabbed us and left black streaks on our bare legs. We wound up descending on Rabanal from the fields above the town, instead of along the road that entered with decorum from below. No doubt we were quite a sight, had there been anyone to see us; but our only fanfare was the lazy barking of a single dog from a nice, dry doorway, at which we gazed with envy.

For lunch we found shelter with a few other pilgrims in the one large room of an abandoned house. Picking our way gingerly across the warped floorboards to claim a corner of the room, we extracted our lunch — tomatoes, cheese, cucumbers, bread — in pieces from our backpacks and set it out on a window ledge, chatting with five young Spaniards who were snuggled in their sleeping bags playing cards. In another corner, a couple in their thirties feasted like royalty on steaming apple tarts from a hamper brought by jovial relatives. We munched our stone-cold sandwiches, eyeing the tarts wistfully, longing to stay in this creaky, chilly haven. Twenty kilometers through rain and wind were beginning to seem like plenty for one day.

However, our fate — along with our warm clothes, sleeping bags, and dinner — lay elsewhere: Theresa was waiting for us somewhere up in Foncebadón. Before we left the refuge, the others tried to dissuade us from going. Didn't we know that Foncebadón was abandoned? Well, we did. But regretfully, pig-headedly, we suited up and pushed back out into the gale.

And a gale it had become. For the next six kilometers we struggled up that mountain through a tempest so stiff that it could have set a cathedral dancing like a birthday balloon. Ponchos plastered to our bodies, we bent double into the wind to avoid being blown back down the mountain. I might have relished the elemental fight, but my cold legs seized at the

24

climb and now I found myself falling behind, lurching slowly through the storm. Finally I stumbled on yet another slick rock and halted, momentarily overwhelmed.

I wasn't going to make it. I sank down on a stone by the side of the trail, gutted. This rock would be my new home. I'd pull my poncho down to my toes and hunker down like a turtle. There were cookies in my pack, but not very many. Once I ran out of food I would gracefully expire by the side of the path. Future pilgrims could build me a nice cairn with some of these rocks. I would become the Patron Saint of the Footsore. Pilgrims would leave me votive offerings of fresh band-aids and *galletas* spread with Nocilla chocolate hazelnut spread, and I'd bless their boots and miracle away their blisters.

Delusional and deafened by the wind, I needed a moment to notice that someone had loomed up ahead of me on the track. Water coursed off the brim of his floppy hat and ran in rivulets down his dark-green poncho — Dad. Skidding carefully down the muddy trail, he was reaching out toward me with his *bordón*. My canonization would have to be postponed. Abandoning my restful plans, I hauled myself up off the Rock of Despair and grasped the end of the staff. Dad kept hold of the other end and, turning back into the gale, he hauled me, step by step, up that mountain. We plodded into Foncebadón like a one-car freight train, its determined engine steaming steadily up the grade. And there, tired and triumphant, we reunited with our disheveled companions. We all stood there panting at the foot of the abandoned village giggling dementedly and baring our teeth in the wind.

Foncebadón sits on one side of a saddle between mountains, so to enter the village required still more climbing, but thankfully, my legs had at last loosened with use. Giddily, wearily, the line of us trailed onward and upward through the long, thin village, peering through the rain at small ruined houses. Now and then we'd pass another heap of masonry and take a rough inventory: was this our evening's shelter? Roof caved in; floor rotted out; walls overgrown with trees; we could only hope not. Every few minutes we'd stop to chant, "*Uno, dos, tres*" and scream thinly into the wind, "THERESA!!"

At last we found her, huddled in the car outside the very last house in the village. Gratefully we climbed inside the little house — climbed, because the stairs were missing, as was the door, and anything in the windows that might once have prevented the outside from coming in, which it was doing with great energy. On the plus side, the roof was intact. There was also a floor, covered with a great heap of broken bricks and rubble. In one corner were the hopeful remains of a banked fire, left for us (Theresa explained) by a pair of French pilgrims who had lunched with her that afternoon. Diego took it upon himself to breathe life back into the glowing heap of coals, and wandered out into the fog to find more wood to bring back and dry. He also dragged back a small dead tree with a few sad, spindly branches left; we set this up in the corner next to the fire, draped it with our soggy socks and shirts, and dubbed it "the Christmas tree." Clearing away the rubble in front of the most solid wall, we spread our sleeping bags over the thick coat of white dust left behind.

Then three or four people began trying to construct a brick barrier in the west window, whence entered the gale with the greatest violence. Three times they got the wall partially constructed before it fell in with a resounding crash; but the fourth time it appeared to hold. Eventually the lowest part of the window was blocked with bricks, and the entire thing more or less covered with Diego's blue poncho. The poncho was secured by tying it to roof beams above and to some of the bigger rocks on the floor; piling bricks on its protruding edges; and leaning against it a contraption made of *bordones*, reinforced with bricks. It was alarming to look at, but it cut the wind a good deal, in spite of the frantic flapping of the poncho's sides and hood. After dragging over flat rocks for seats, we huddled around the fire, playing cards and reading, and, when our hands thawed, writing. I stretched out my sore legs. A few people curled up in their sleeping bags to doze and conserve a little body heat; the indefatigable ventured out into the foggy village to poke around in the half-ruined houses. The mysterious son, Angel, was spotted in the rain with his sheep.

Having exhausted the evening's entertainments, we

gathered around the fire at 8:00 for an early dinner, which turned out to be a real feast. Linda, who had a genius for knowing just when a treat would be needed, had long ago earned our devotion and the title *"Nuestra Señora del Chocolate"* — Our Lady of Chocolate. Having anticipated the hard day and the chilly night, *Nuestra Señora* had given Theresa extra money and a list of exotic items to buy for the evening repast. We spread some dry-ish ponchos over the soft brick dust and Theresa began laying out the goodies: bread and cheese, fruit and yogurt, olives and cucumber; our picnic staples. But the delicacies kept coming: fruit juice and wine. Ham and *morcilla* (blood sausage). Tins of sardines, tuna, and mussels. A salad made out of canned peas, chickpeas, and pears, garnished with onion and sweet red pepper. The decadence was dizzying. For dessert we consumed an entire jar of Nocilla spread on crackers.

Then there was nothing left but to crawl into our sleeping bags, thump our duffel-pillows till the shoes and three-ring binders were toward the bottom, and go to sleep. As the rain blew fitfully in through a nearby window I drew my poncho up over my sleeping bag, propped up my backpack so the scallop shell made a little ledge, and laid my glasses there. The windbreak over the windows slapped and rattled, and a light mist of rain settled on my hair. Closing my eyes I rolled into sleep like a hibernating bear.

In the morning I woke early to a dripping silence. The open windows and door framed nothing but cloud, as though we'd ascended during the night. I turned over and snuggled back to sleep.

By 9:00 we'd breakfasted on fruit and *magdalenas*, reclaimed our ponchos, and slapped the brick dust off our sleeping bags. The white-out showed no signs of dissolving, but as we peered out the empty doorframe into the featureless fog a backpacked figure floated suddenly into view and then dematerialized back into the whiteness. Another ghostly hiker soon passed, and another; in all, a line of perhaps twenty pilgrims, the most we'd ever seen, appeared and disappeared almost silently along the track outside. Bidding our hovel farewell we slipped out into the mist behind them.

We climbed for half an hour and the cloud thinned out enough that we could see a small mountain of scree just off the trail. We had reached the *Cruz de Ferro*, a landmark long famous among pilgrims. The tall stone pole supporting the small iron cross was almost buried under a cairn of stones centuries in the making. Faithful pilgrims, by the thousands in medieval times and sporadically ever since, carried stones from home until they could drop their symbolic burden at the foot of this cross. We tossed our tiny, secular stones upon the pile, scaled the sliding heap to have our pictures taken, and then descended to follow the trail through the pass.

On we wandered like a lost tribe through the muffling cloud. The wind rushed in my ears. Faintly through the drizzle and mist I could make out a hazy figure ahead of me on the trail. It seemed we walked endlessly in our separate cloud cocoons over the same shrubby ground covering of purple, green, and yellow, with a lot of red earth and gray rock in between. I could tell we were through the pass when the path began sloping slightly downward. Sometimes my feet hit paved road; sometimes I followed yellow blazes and cairns down the precarious mountainside itself. Occasionally I sang to keep myself company. Somewhere up ahead I could hear Dad singing too, and then I turned an invisible corner and just like that I was out of the cloud. I stopped short, blinking at the abrupt change in perspective and depth: laid out before me was a staggeringly expansive view of the valleys far below, with beyond them the mountains of Galicia.

One by one my *compañeros* emerged from the cloud and stopped, stunned motionless by the view. I stretched and pushed back my hood. People took off their packs and we lingered for a bit, passing around snacks and marveling at this lifting of the veil. Dad handed me a mandarin and I ate it, gazing happily out at the suddenly wide world. I had come so far. My legs felt strong and ready. The long road wound away beneath us westward toward Santiago. For a little while at least, it was all downhill from here.

ALL SIGNS POINT TO YES

Jessica Hickam Roffe

Why did I walk the Camino? I am not a hiker. I am not an outdoor enthusiast. But in May of 2001 I did what few other 20-year-old Americans decide to do on their summer break — I walked 300 miles across Spain. The decision to take on the Camino was a surprisingly easy one to make. As soon as I saw the description in my college's May course list, I knew I wanted to do it. So, why did I walk?

First, I wanted to find clarity in my life. I spent my freshman year in a long distance relationship that ended that summer, so when I returned to school for my sophomore year I was struggling to create my new identity. I made a lot of poor choices and was frustrated with who I was becoming. I needed clarity. I needed to find myself. I needed to redirect myself before it was too late. Both required removing distractions from my life. I thought, if all I have to do each day is get up, put on my boots and start walking, surely I'd have time to think. I was right. I walked for about 6 hours each day. In the beginning I walked with my friend, who was also doing the Camino. We were sounding boards for each other. It's amazing what you hear yourself saying when you've been talking for 6 hours straight for 6 days in a row. You catch yourself admitting fears, hopes and dreams out loud that you'd never even admitted to yourself. As though we were on matching clocks, everyone ran out of things to talk about by 10 days in. We just wanted to walk. Alone. Alone with our empty minds that had been drained of everything we'd ever wanted to say. By the next day we were ready for companionship again as the Camino continued on.

I also thought I would come back with a six-pack of abs if I walked 300 miles in less than 30 days. Surprisingly I came back looking the same, but with blisters and funky tan lines. I'm sure it had some health benefit though, surely?

The trip also offered a sense of accomplishment. "Hey, Jessica, what'd you do this summer?" "Oh, you know, the usual, I walked 300 miles across Spain. What'd you do?" "Doesn't matter … wasn't nearly as cool as that." I will always have "2001 May Intensive Learning, Camino de Santiago, Spain" listed on my résumé.

And when I find myself doubting what I can do I just remind myself of the crazy summer I walked 300 miles across Spain.

The experience that was the most meaningful to me started at the cathedral of Santiago. My mother had asked me to buy her a rosary made of rose petals at the beginning of my journey and have it blessed by a priest inside the cathedral in Santiago at the end of my journey. I learned how to say "Bless this, please" in Spanish and recited it over and over to myself until I reached the priest. I handed him the rosary, repeated my newly learned phrase, and he blessed it for me. After giving my mom the rosary, I realized how much I wished I had gotten one for myself. Years later when I got engaged, my mother gave the rosary back to me. She knew how much more it meant to me than it could ever mean to her. Seven years after I completed the Camino de Santiago, I carried the rosary down the aisle, wrapped around my bridal bouquet, as I married my college sweetheart.

As you enter the cathedral in Santiago, there is a marble pillar carved with the Tree of Jesse, which, based on a passage from the book of Isaiah, describes the descent of Jesus from Jesse of Bethlehem. For hundreds of years, pilgrims have been placing their hand on the pillar and saying a prayer. This pillar has been touched so many times that a hand print has actually been eroded into the marble about an inch deep. Placing my hand inside the handprint formed by the hundreds of thousands of pilgrims before me instantly brought tears to my eyes. We had all made the journey. I now stood in the footsteps of those who passed before me. Their strength was my strength. We shared a bond that could only be understood by those who had walked in our shoes.

The physical effects that I suffered from hiking a long-distance trail could have all been prevented. So please, take into account the lessons I learned the hard way:

#1 Don't be a prick — use a stick!!! We thought that since we had small backpacks we didn't need walking sticks. We were wrong and my knees paid the price. I couldn't even sit with my legs crossed for a month after the Camino and still deal with pain when I exercise heavily.

#2 Break-in your walking shoes. Despite constant reminders to break my shoes in, I only wore them once before the Camino and they ended up being too small. I developed at least one blister a day.

Now, nearly a decade later, I miss the days of just waking up and following yellow arrows and scallop shells across the countryside. The life of a pilgrim didn't require a lot of decisions. The path you needed to take was clearly marked out for you. Oh, how I wish "grown-up" life were that easy. Without my yellow arrows, how am I supposed to know that the direction I'm headed in is the right one? Now the decisions are all up to me. Or maybe the signs just aren't as clear. They require a little more soul searching, a little more faith and a lot more praying. But just like on the Camino, no matter which paths you choose to take, God is always with you. ¡Buen Camino!

ON STOLEN SILVER AND BORROWED TIME

Dave Whitson

The most famous young pilgrim on the medieval Camino de Santiago, a German teenager named Hugonell, failed to reach his intended destination. As the story goes, Hugonell and his parents reached Santo Domingo de la Calzada where they found an inn for the night. The innkeeper's daughter had indecent designs for the youthful pilgrim; devout in purpose, however, he was little moved by her flirtatious advances. Lust gave way to bitterness, and the girl hatched a scheme to punish his rejection of her, framing him for the theft of the inn's silver. Ultimately, Hugonell was found guilty and sentenced to hanging. St. James, however, intervened - keeping the boy alive and healthy while dangling from the gallows outside of Santo Domingo, until his parents returned from Santiago de Compostela and found him laughing and waving.

This story of Hugonell is typically upheld as an example of St. James's protection of pilgrims on his sacred road. Anyone who has walked the Camino with a young companion, however, knows how much truth is reflected in the cheerful portrayal of Hugonell, who remains jovial in the most dubious of circumstances. The pilgrimage experience is one of tremendous personal volatility, with elevation changes in mood far sharper than the trail to and from O Cebreiro. Maintaining equanimity in the midst of crisis or even discomfort is every bit as miraculous an outcome as a saint holding you up by the boots. And young people seem to have more capacity for that than adults.

I walked my first Camino — alone, or at least as alone as one ever is on the Camino Francés — in 2002. I returned in 2004 with a group of high school students and two teachers. I was a recent college graduate, preparing for my own career as a teacher, and eager to give high schoolers the experience from which I had benefited so much. Since then, I have returned to Spain with three more groups — twice more on the Francés and once on the Norte/Primitivo — along with one group trip to Italy on the Via Francigena. All told, I have taken 45 high schoolers on pilgrimage. Fortunately, none have been accused of stealing silver, though there was an unfortunate incident with some sugar cubes in a bar in Foncebadón...

On every trip, in every group, like Hugonell we were lifted by Santiago - whether the saint or the destination. And, I was frequently supported by the positivity and eagerness of my students. Similarly, the miracle story of Hugonell and Santiago existed only because of their shared contributions. A failure on either end would have resulted in a much more dour return to Santo Domingo for Hugonell's parents. Hugonell's faith, persistence, and devotion earned the blessings of St. James.

He also represents a model for reflecting on the pilgrimage experience. Hugonell engaged in the act of pilgrimage with his parents — and remained celibate in Santo Domingo — because of a core faith that inspired his actions. His faith was rewarded and reflected in a miracle and his experience is also encapsulated in a relic (in this case it is an unusual one, still alive and clucking — two live chickens housed in a glass chamber in the town's cathedral). And, though the story concludes with the miracle, one must assume that his initial faith was deepened and transformed through his personal contact with St. James. Those four components — the initial faith, the miracle, the relic, and the altered or renewed faith — are central elements of the pilgrimage experience and all have been evident in my students' experiences, as well as my own, on the Camino de Santiago. Reflecting on these components, I believe, helps us to better see what the journey can mean specifically for young pilgrims.

INITIAL FAITH

All pilgrims start with an initial faith — the core beliefs that compel them to shoulder the backpack, lace up the boots, and stride confidently (some more so than others) out their front door. This doesn't have to be religious or even spiritual in nature. But, walking 500 miles across Spain is not an idle endeavor, pursued without a second thought. The seed might be small when planted, but over time it grows wildly, pushing into every corner of the mind. Pilgrims walk the Camino because not walking the Camino is not an option.

When I first walked the Camino Francés, I was motivated primarily by the desire to experience history and to live a life not radically unlike those preceding me on the route a millennium earlier (aside from the Gore-Tex). I am not a religious man, but I also felt a strong pull toward the Camino because of its spiritual significance. Growing up in the Seattle area, a staunchly liberal and secular part of the United States, I had cultivated a hearty sense of skepticism and looked at the devout in a critical way. Even while dispensing platitudes about the perceived evils of organized religion, though, I grew increasingly conscious of the inherent unfairness of such a stance, especially for one separated to the extent that I was from the phenomenon. I wanted to know — in a real and authentic way — what it meant to be Catholic, to be Christian, and I hoped that I could find that on pilgrimage.

While older than the students I would eventually lead on the Camino, I was still a young *peregrino*, only 23. Meanwhile, most of my fellow travelers, as well as the people I read about in published journals, were middle-aged or retired. In many cases, they had a lifetime of experiences — and, sometimes, a lifetime of regrets or bad habits — and they needed the walking, the solitude, to sort through those events in order to find closure, peace, and perhaps a new path.

I could see and appreciate the relevance of the Camino experience to their circumstances. But, I also recognized immediately the critical part it could play in the lives of teenagers, situated at a pivotal moment in their own lives as they prepared for the leap to adulthood, university, career, personal freedom. Driven practically from birth to build and bolster their academic resume, to fill their schedules with sufficient commitments to display their "well-roundedness," to meet the burden of parental (and personal) expectation, what time is left for the development of a sense of self-identity? What opportunities are there for meaningful human interaction, as opposed to a quick text or Facebook message? When are they left to their own devices to entertain themselves, to stimulate and reward their own curiosity?

Wouldn't we all like to be able to go back to that moment in our lives and take a timeout? To that moment, when the infinite forks of possible lives splintered endlessly in front of us. To that moment, when clarity and conviction seemed all too elusive, or misleading in their abundance, but now to be given the critical piece of advice, the head-clearing epiphany, the yellow arrow to guide us forward...

The yellow arrows! A golden contradiction — never do we feel more free than we do on pilgrimage, but never are we more dependent and beholden to external forces. It seems a devil's bargain, to sacrifice partial freedom in exchange for absolute freedom. Only through simplification, though, can we pierce the outer shell, cut through the concentric layers of responsibility, expectation, and self-deception to find what lies beneath. On pilgrimage, life is exposed, laid bare of all adornment — you wake, walk, eat, sleep. The only critical decision is whether to stop in one town or continue to the next. Everything else is discretionary.

What initial faith did my students bring on the Camino? Like me, few were religious. Many were skeptical. Most were nervous, to varying degrees, as I was on my first walk. The most common characteristic I have seen in my students is a commitment, a devotion really, to the group from the very outset of the experience. Whatever personal weaknesses they might possess, whatever concerns they might carry, they have always been dedicated to one another. And that, ultimately, strikes me as the defining characteristic of a pilgrim — in the pursuit of a heightened sense of self, the level of selflessness is elevated to new heights. Even those who begin walking as individuals quickly find themselves, if open to it, connected to a pack, bonded in shared identity with the strangers around them.

MIRACLES

As the Hugonell story illustrates, pilgrimage and miracles have a close relationship and it seems perfectly reasonable to hope for divine influence while on a sacred road. Even more, that hope is often confirmed by the individual pilgrim experience. Many, upon arrival in Santiago, can recall a moment of remarkable coincidence, in which needs were met almost as swiftly as they were voiced.

Over the course of traveling with four student groups on the Camino, I've seen many touched by miracles. Early on the first trip, two students were struggling with illness and injury, suffering as they approached the ascent to the windmills after Cizur Menor. To their surprise, they were greeted by three *peregrinas* under a tree, who immediately provided medication, supplies, and even fresh cherries. On another occasion, we were bitterly disappointed to arrive in Negreira as fireworks exploded over town, auguring a fiesta day — and, by extension, the closure of the supermarkets we had counted on to provide supplies for our next three dinners. However, shortly after leaving Negreira, sulking as we walked, we happened upon a bar unmentioned in the guide, a bar that contained a small grocery. It was basic, but again, it met our needs. Sometimes, the Camino goes even further. One student, Jim had spent several days talking about how much he missed hearing his favorite band. As we sat in the *albergue* in Redecilla del Camino, though, he heard a car pull up in front, playing one of that band's CDs. Jim ran to the window and called down to the driver, telling the driver how much he liked the band - and the driver promptly ejected the CD and tossed it up to Jim!

These three stories are all clear cases of coincidence; I'll leave the debate over whether a divine hand is behind the action to another day. Some events, though, are more stunning and inexplicable.

Laura decided to walk the Camino despite a bad hip, injured playing soccer the previous fall. Despite a full commitment to rehabilitation, it remained problematic and had limited her opportunities to participate in training hikes. Our hope was that, once she crossed the Pyrenees — which we knew would be agonizing — the hip would gradually strengthen over the course of the walk. We counted on the largely flat Meseta, in particular, as a place where she would experience a respite of sorts. Now, this plan wouldn't have been an option for many people. Few would want to subject themselves to such constant discomfort and, as a leader, I wouldn't want to put someone in a situation where they were likely to fail. Laura, however, was persistent, determined, stubborn -- pick your adjective. The point is that she would go as far as her body would take her. Turned out, her body took her as far as Burgos.

While walking from the center of Burgos to the municipal *albergue*, Laura discovered that her hip had weakened dramatically. Our hope was that an afternoon of rest and icing would help matters and, as noted, the Meseta promised easier walking ahead. The next morning, Laura and I departed early, with two other students, to ensure that she could walk at a comfortable pace. However, shortly before Villalbilla, her body gave way and she dropped to the ground. She could barely walk, and certainly not with her backpack. We staggered into the village, called for a taxi, and transported her to our day's destination, Hontanas.

The other trip leaders and I sat down with Laura. I told her that we would taxi her forward as long as she believed her hip would improve and allow her to walk again. But, I added, she should prepare for the fact that her Camino was probably over. Laura was not pleased with that statement.

Laura taxied through most of the Meseta. However, she was able to shoulder her pack and make the short walk from Mansilla de las Mulas to León without any ill effect. Still, we were nervous. The mountains loomed and threatened to make whatever improvements she had enjoyed short-lived.

But Laura was done with taxis. From León onward, she made every walk, covered every kilometer, leaving a

42

trail of melted ice cubes and empty ibuprofen packs behind her. Amazingly, she not only completed each walk, she got stronger. Her recovery — her rebirth, really — culminated just outside of Portomarín. Galicia brings many new walkers, including a number of larger tour groups. They are, without question, pilgrims like us and as welcome to the Camino as we are. But they can present a challenge for those who started farther out, as they often proceed slowly and in large bunches. As we departed Portomarín, we saw 30 or 40 pilgrims ahead of us, all wearing matching yellow arrow shirts and filling the trail. With one look, we crossed over to the road and started running, uphill, past the group. Laura stayed with us step for step, an act unthinkable on the first day of the trip, never mind a week earlier in Mansilla.

Laura completed the Camino, stronger than she had started, as miraculous an act as I have seen on any pilgrimage.

The Camino teaches us to be optimistic. The road will provide. Desires dressed as needs will be exposed and dismissed. True needs will be met. Challenges that seem overwhelming will be overcome. Perhaps the most miraculous aspect of pilgrimage, though, is learning that human kindness, personal resilience, and the joys of simplicity are not miracles in their own right but immediate and accessible should we be open to them.

RELICS

Traditionally, pilgrims were either motivated by the pursuit of relics or found their own experiences deepened in meaning through their encounter with physical objects that possess or become imbued with special significance. The most obvious example of this, of course, are the physical remains of St. James said to rest in the cathedral of Santiago. Many pilgrims today, religious or not, still derive great personal importance from the scallop shell that they tie to their packs or around their necks. Beyond that, the act of walking elevates the relationship between the pilgrim and the human geography of the Way. We feel the towns, the churches, even the cups of *café con leche* differently on foot than we do when arrived at through motorized transport.

With a largely secular group, the traditional relics give pause but lack the same meaning that they provide to a Catholic audience. But, the arched walls surrounding Eunate, the Órbigo bridge, the *horreos* and *pallozas* of Galicia — these all provide physical conduits through which we connect with the history of the land and the lives of the pilgrims preceding us.

The most potent relics for my students — and admittedly, I am stretching the term a bit here — are the ones connecting them not with past Christian saints but rather with their own past lives at home. Separated from what they have always known, from how they have lived, from the material objects always at their disposal, my students, like all other pilgrims, have been given the distance to consider the importance of those objects and practices. Many prove to be disposable. Others are revealed to be integral to the individual's identity.

Hannah was a violinist. She couldn't recall ever having gone a week without playing, let alone a month. She worried about the separation anxiety heading into the trip, and the absence resonated more loudly with each passing day in Spain. And then we arrived in León.

The León Cathedral is, of course, one of the most remarkable structures on the Camino, due in large part to its spectacular stained glass windows that fill the building with an explosion of color. On an ordinary day, the cathedral would be extraordinary. This was not a normal day, though; it was a wedding day. And, as the soon to be married couple concluded their nuptials, a small string orchestra at the back of the room played for the crowd, the notes echoing throughout the cathedral, intermingling with the colors to produce a symphony for the senses.

Admittedly, the wedding alone had already made some of the girls a little teary-eyed. But when Hannah saw the violinist — and, more specifically, the violin — the wedding was forgotten. She stared in longing, in anticipation, in love — she stared. And slowly, she built up the courage, assembling her Spanish words to compose a request on which her over-sized hopes rested. As the musicians concluded and began packing their gear, Hannah approached and asked the violinist if she could play the woman's violin, just for a moment.

Before long, Hannah stood outside the cathedral, violin raised to her chin, and all of us sat around her, listening to her play. The plaza is a busy place, with restaurants, children playing, cameras clicking and flashing, but the cliché is true -- the world outside our circle was silenced, then disappeared altogether. I imagine that even we ceased to exist for Hannah, as muscle memory guided her fingers along the strings, while tears streamed down her face.

Behold the power that lies in a single object: to merge the past and present, to identify or reinforce priorities, to connect us with the divine, to unite a group in peaceful harmony.

ALTERED FAITH

All pilgrims return home with an altered or renewed faith. Some, though rare, depart St. Jean as atheists or tourists and arrive in Santiago as devout Catholics. Many more experience profound transformations in their sense of self. Perpetual homebodies find their self-imposed limits shattered by this remarkable physical accomplishment. More often than not, the changes initiated require time to process and recognize; only in hindsight can we fully assess the impact of a specific event. This is why many pilgrims consider the arrival in Santiago to represent not the conclusion of the journey but rather the beginning.

Some lessons are readily identified. While Laura's success was reflected in her ability to walk faster, and even to run, other students realized the need to slow down. By sprinting through stages, they earned themselves an extra couple of hours of sitting in line outside of the *albergue*, waiting for it to open. By slackening their pace, they could actually experience the places through which they were walking. The aphorism about the journey and the destination holds special truth on the Camino.

Other students discovered the value of taking chances, of being assertive. It's easy to hide in a group, to not form connections with other pilgrims. When we did, though, our pilgrimage experience was significantly altered. The artificiality of those things dividing us — language, nationality, culture, religion — becomes all the more apparent when you realize how much can be communicated with someone with whom you share no words and how close you can become to that person.

The beauty, though, is that the greatest impact, the most powerful changes, may not yet have taken place and may still not for many years. We are young, our possible lives lie ahead, and how many of those paths now have yellow arrows pointing boldly forward! In making and completing our pilgrimage — and thus, in discovering more clearly our own identities, in becoming more optimistic and persistent, and in a growing openness to the people and opportunities around us — we equip ourselves with the map, the compass, and the guidebook that allow us to pursue our own paths with confidence and faith.

So long as we treat all innkeepers' daughters nicely along the way...

A JOURNEY YET UNFINISHED

Nicholas Hoekstra

A pilgrim on the Camino de Santiago told me upon the completion of my 300-kilometer journey from León, "Celebrate tonight and enjoy yourself. It will be three weeks before you appreciate what you've accomplished." Two weeks and more of experiences cannot be condensed into the single moment of entering the Cathedral of Santiago. Now, more than six years later and ten thousand kilometers from Spain, the thoughts and feelings I experienced while walking the Camino are still present in my mind. The path I began walking on May 14th, 2004, is one that I continue today. The Cathedral of Santiago was a stop along the way — one which I have revisited since and will return to again — but the road has continued for as long as I have cared to walk.

I first heard about the Camino de Santiago in a Spanish history class at the University of Michigan. I was in my sophomore year and had only recently decided to take my interest in the Spanish language and make it my focus of studies. The graduate student leading our discussion group mentioned that two professors were organizing a trip to Spain for the following summer to hike the Camino. I immediately turned to a friend in the class and said, "I'm going with them." There was no question in my mind that I could miss this opportunity to experience Spain in such a unique manner. The idea that I might be turned down for the group never even occurred to me.

Two professors were putting together a group of fourteen students to walk the Camino de Santiago as part of the Global

Intercultural Exchange for Undergraduates (GIEU) program; a program which seeks to build community on an international level through work and travel. The group that was to go to Spain would hike the 300 kilometers from León to Santiago de Compostela. Along the way, students were to keep a daily journal of their thoughts and experiences while walking this ancient and, for many, very spiritual pilgrimage. It was also suggested that, each night, the students should invite another pilgrim or small group of pilgrims to dine with them. Through interviews and daily interactions while hiking, students would gain an understanding for the reasons people had for walking.

The professors later told me that they had their doubts when I first presented myself as a candidate for the 2004 GIEU program. They worried not only about how I would manage walking the Camino when the path turned rough and slippery, but how I would handle matters of daily life while staying in new and unfamiliar surroundings.

They had never imagined that a blind student would ask to join them on their hike. While the Camino is wide and smooth in parts — especially near larger towns and cities — it becomes a rocky climb in the mountains. When it rains, as it often does in May in Galicia, the trail becomes muddy and difficult for even sighted hikers to navigate. There was also the question of how a blind pilgrim would get around the communal living quarters in the various *albergues* where he would be sleeping each night.

At the age of seven, an undetected brain tumor began to put increasing pressure on my optic nerve. For months I experienced severe migraines. Doctors ran a battery of tests from CT-scans to MRI's but were unable to determine what was causing my headaches. It was finally a graduate student who came across a similar case in a medical history. Due to a blockage in my spinal column, cerebral fluid was unable to drain off the brain. This fluid was essentially pooling behind the optic nerve, putting greater and greater pressure upon both nerve and brain. What began as severe headaches soon became vision loss. By the time the tumor was discovered, immediate action had to be taken in order to avoid brain damage. This immediate action came in the form of two laser surgeries — one on either eye — which, though further damaging the optic nerve, took pressure off the brain. An LP-shunt was also put in my stomach, near the base of my spine, which would drain fluid from my head and help to relieve pressure. Though the tumor dissipated, I was left completely blind.

"I'm going with them," is a statement indicative of the attitude with which I have always approached life as a visually impaired person. I have never let blindness stop me from accomplishing any dream or desire. The professors later said that it was this attitude, combined with the fact that I had previously visited Spain and stayed with a family for a short time that earned me a place on the 2004 GIEU Camino de Santiago Program.

In our modern world of North Face raincoats and Gortex boots; when flights connect Paris to Madrid and trains commute daily between Madrid and Santiago de Compostela, what has kept the magic of walking a 1,000-year-old pilgrimage alive? Something more than the promise of absolution, surely. Hiking the Camino de Santiago is a truly unique opportunity. Religious in its origins, the Camino goes beyond its Christian roots to provide a spiritual experience for people of varying faiths or of none. Life becomes somehow simpler when your worldly possessions consist of — or are limited to — those items you can carry in a backpack. When your only "job" is that of arriving to the next town, your mind is free to view matters in a different light.

Admittedly, the Camino wasn't always a scenic stroll. Bandits, disease, and severe weather were very real concerns for pilgrims traveling in medieval times. The pilgrimage to Santiago was a journey one made but once in a lifetime, and the length of the Camino was spent in meditation and prayer. Perhaps due to the serious nature of this journey, an attitude of charity developed along the Camino. The characteristic cockle shell was originally gathered from the shores of Finisterre as proof of having made the journey, but later pilgrims carried shells as a sign that they were traveling to Santiago. This provided them both protection from thieves as well as refuge and free meals in churches.

Though present-day pilgrims don't face the same dangers as their medieval counterparts, the Camino de Santiago is not an easy undertaking. Many people underestimate the difficulty of walking twenty to thirty kilometers in one day, only to wake and continue the next. For some, it's a challenge just to leave behind the creature comforts of a normal life. Pilgrims are not always guaranteed a bed; more often than not, a thin mat on the floor is the best one can expect. For others, detaching themselves from their busy lives is the most difficult test of all. But though the challenges along the Camino have changed, the sense of community and charity has remained. The Camino provides the backdrop upon which our own, personal weaknesses can sometimes take shape, but the strength and support to overcome these obstacles can also be found. This support might come in the form of a hug at the end of the day or, as I witnessed in one case, an outpouring of concern when a fellow pilgrim had fallen.

When I started the Camino, I was uncertain how I would manage to do things for myself. Needing to depend upon other people for assistance has always been a very personal struggle. Since the time I lost my sight, I've been fiercely protective of my own independence. Though I had moved away from home for university, I was constantly surrounded by classmates and professors. Their presence made it easy for me to maintain a sense of independence while still having people I could rely on. Walking the Camino, however, made me consider the reality of a future in which I planned to travel and live abroad. How would I move from place to place? How would I eat and sleep and find all those things necessary to survive? The most difficult question though, was how I would deal with people's reactions to my blindness.

As well as providing me with the realization of the difficulties in a future of travel abroad, the Camino de Santiago also gave me the chance to test something of my independence in a foreign environment. Each night we stayed in a different *albergue*, the buildings constantly changing and challenging me to adapt quickly. I also found myself surrounded by a foreign language and was often forced to express myself with what limited vocabulary I had. Despite these difficulties, however, I found myself capable of becoming acclimated to every new setting. Each day I would quickly learn the layout of the *albergue* so I could be self-sufficient. I learned to observe the movements of the people around me, listening closely and making note of where chairs, tables, and even stairs were located. The first thing I would do upon arriving at each *albergue* was to ask the location of the bathroom. After that, everything seemed simple. Even finding my sleeping mat or bed was easier than I had expected. I would often put my backpack at the foot of the mattress so, if I wasn't sure where I was sleeping, I could subtly let my hand brush past beds as I walked until I came to my own.

From the first night, I was delighted by the seemingly endless opportunities to speak Spanish. Fellow pilgrims were always interested in speaking with our group and I often acted as an interpreter. These pilgrims were always very patient and helped me learn to express myself with what vocabulary I knew. I developed a much greater confidence in my language abilities, the culmination of which came one day when the pilgrim with whom I was walking passed out from dehydration. We had been pushing ourselves more than necessary and my friend had not been drinking enough water. When she started to feel chills, despite the mid-day heat, I told her to sit down. She then fainted. I was faced with the challenge of explaining the situation to passing pilgrims without knowing the words "faint" or "dehydrated".

The aspect of my doing the Camino de Santiago that most worried other people — namely, the hiking — was quickly shown to be a needless concern. Growing up with somewhat reckless friends, who didn't think twice about pulling me along into forests and swamps, had accustomed me to walking on uncertain footing. I had also been training intensively in the martial arts and I quickly found myself leading the group, walking with anyone who could keep pace. It was for this reason, perhaps, that I found the protective nature of other pilgrims so difficult to comprehend.

The first time a person went out of her way to help me came as we were leaving the café where we had eaten a mid-morning breakfast on the third or fourth day of our hike. As our group of sixteen pilgrims adjusted backpacks and prepared to walk, the owner — a small woman of sixty or so years — hustled out of the bar with a tall walking staff in her hand. She rushed over and presented me with the cane. It was a beautiful wooden staff, polished smooth with a metal point for better traction. She said I would need the extra support in the mountains.

At this time, other members of our group were already experiencing some knee and ankle pains, so I carried the staff until we were out of sight of the café. I then gave the walking stick to another member of the group who needed it more. Though I was struck by the woman's kind gesture, I was also bothered by the fact that I had been singled out. This was not the only time I would be given special treatment despite being in better shape than other pilgrims in my group.

The arrival to Galicia and the first Galician town, O Cebreiro, is heralded by a long day's hike, ending with a strenuous seven-kilometer climb through the mountains. To make matters worse, this stage of the Camino becomes a race in the summer when space is limited and pilgrims rush to finish their day's march and lay claim to one of the few beds at the *albergue*. I went with one of the professors on the afternoon of our arrival to O Cebreiro to see if there was space available for our group. The climb had been difficult for some of our members and they were suffering from severe blisters and tendonitis. The last thing we expected was the brusque way the *hospitalera* checking pilgrims into the *albergue* treated us. She off-handedly told us that there were no beds available for such a large group and that they didn't cater to tourists. We explained that we represented a university in the United States and that we were walking from León to Santiago. The *hospitalera* had no interest in listening to our story, finally only offering to "make an exception for the blind person." At this, I lost my temper. I told her that the "blind person" was perfectly happy sleeping on the floor, but that we had friends who were sick and really needed a chance to recover. Other pilgrims who were witness to our discussion with the *hospitalera* finally came forward to offer their own beds. In the end, we were given three places for the pilgrims who were suffering most in our group, while the rest of us, myself included, slept on the floor in a side room.

The condescending nature of the woman in O Cebreiro left me feeling frustrated and unhappy with people's attitudes toward blindness. Whereas I could fight condescension, however, the reaction I found hardest to understand was admiration. As we came closer to Santiago, word of our group spread. The fact that we were all very friendly and obviously interested in Spanish culture and in the lives of the pilgrims we encountered made a great impression on both pilgrims and *hospitaleros* alike. At a few *albergues*, workers were thoughtful enough to call ahead to neighboring towns and ask fellow *hospitaleros* to reserve places for us. Along with word of our group spread word of the "blind pilgrim," and on one occasion I was even greeted by name as we entered a town.

A few days before arriving to Santiago, I was approached by an elderly man at the *albergue* where we were staying. The man came forward hesitantly and began speaking to me in a shaky voice. I was confused at first, and unable to understand what the pilgrim was trying to say. Despite this, he took my hand and stood with me for a moment, finally beginning to cry. Another pilgrim explained to me later that the man was overcome by emotion at the sight of a blind pilgrim. I was also overcome by emotion and almost began crying myself, but for a completely different reason.

As is the case with most college students, I was very young and largely untested by the world. I had lost my sight as a child and never really had come to terms with what that meant. I struggled on a daily basis with my own fears and doubts — as do all people — and felt the need to prove myself an equal to my sighted peers. Success, in my mind, was to blend in with the crowd. Rather than blend in, however, I was admired for my accomplishments and set apart; congratulated for achieving things other people took in stride. It seemed that no matter what I did, I would always be viewed in terms of the adjectives that described me and never as a "normal" human being. I viewed offers of help as condescending gestures by ignorant people; remarks of admiration were empty words spoken by people who obviously didn't know me; there was nothing admirable about my thoughts and feelings.

I arrived in Santiago on May 30th, 2004, having learned two important things about myself. While walking in the streets and plazas of this beautiful city, I was greeted by pilgrims I had met along my 300-kilometer trek from León. Amid their congratulations and well-wishes, I realized I had the strength to travel and live the life I desired. I had developed the skills necessary to adapt to new and unfamiliar surroundings, and I had found the confidence I needed to explore these places independently. But when I was stopped on the steps outside the Cathedral of Santiago by a French man who placed both his hands on my chest and wanted simply to meet me, I was forced to admit that I was not fully comfortable with how people reacted to my visual impairment. In truth, I was not yet comfortable with my own feelings toward blindness.

My own personal Camino has continued much further than I ever would have imagined in 2004. Eight months after finishing the Camino de Santiago, I studied abroad in Santiago, Chile, where I visited a pilgrim I had met the summer before. After graduating from the University of Michigan, I returned to Spain and lived for two years in Málaga. I volunteered there for the local Xacobea (pilgrimage) association and walked the Camino Portugués in 2007 with a Spanish friend. I now find myself over 10,000 kilometers from Santiago, writing about my experiences in Spain while sitting in a coffee shop in southern Japan. But though I've proved time and again that I can travel and lead an incredible life, I still struggle with my feelings toward blindness and the attitudes other people show when they first meet me. When strangers rush forward to grab my arm as I cross a street or bring me my food pre-cut, I am forced to fight feelings of anger and disappointment. The fact that these people are acting out of kindness only makes matters worse, as I am then plagued by feelings of guilt at my own defensive reactions.

As I search for a way to accept the manner in which people view me without losing my own sense of identity, my thoughts turn frequently to the weeks I spent on the Camino de Santiago. This emotionally intense hike showed me aspects of both the confidence and the self-doubt which I possess. Rather than create these strengths and weaknesses, however, the Camino acted as the backdrop upon which they could be revealed. Though the Camino de Santiago has its official termination at the entrance to the Cathedral of Santiago, I don't believe my journey has ended. For this reason, I intend to return once more to the Camino, but this time as a solitary pilgrim. I feel that putting myself in a situation where I am forced to depend upon strangers for guidance will be the only way I can come to terms with the conflicting emotions I still possess. Walking the Camino alone, I will have no choice but to rely on the aid of other pilgrims and remain patient as they express doubt about my capabilities. I hope to learn that "help" is not always condescension and that "admiration" is a sign of recognition of our efforts, be they the grandest of deeds or the simplest of acts.

A JOURNEY TO ONESELF

Ashleigh Volland Whitmore

The Camino has not left me. In the years since I departed from Spain, this thought has always comforted me, and I return to the recorded memories of my days on the Camino frequently.

In the year following my adventure in the early summer of 2004, I was preparing to enter the real world and quickly found myself searching for a job, a home, new friends, and a new purpose. To ease the anxiety, I intentionally left my diary that chronicled each day spent on the Camino right next to my bed, and I would open the smudged pages often. Even the most incidental experiences from my three weeks on the path would console me, transporting me to a time and place that was both physically challenging and personally fulfilling. When I read my own words again, several years later, I relish the chance to relive the adventure that carried me through the countryside of Spain.

24 mayo, Burgos: "…because all of your sins are washed away when you get to Santiago."

25 mayo, Castrojeriz: "It is inevitable, that everyone knows, that we will be changed somehow upon being received in Santiago."

While on the path, one hears the most frequently asked question, "So why are you doing the Camino?" It's a great opening line, and since everyone is essentially a stranger even as you walk miles alongside each other, it's interesting to know what moves a soul to start walking with the most minimal of supplies for hundreds of miles along an ancient path. The first quote I wrote down came from Clarey, a British girl whom I met on the first day of the Camino. Clarey had a common response, relating to the religious reasons for embarking on a pilgrimage. It was, of course, the primary reason for the Camino in the first place: visiting the place where an enlightened monk was led to find the supposed remains of a key Apostle of Christ: St. James.

I asked this question of strangers even before I asked it of myself. Why did I find myself in *albergues* each night, with or without a mattress, wearing the same dirty socks every day to prevent blisters, and walking without question by the guide of a yellow arrow? Well — and this was my actual answer — because I had to write my college senior thesis. I had no idea what I was really signing up for when I agreed to complete my honors requirements with an extended stay on an old hiking trail; I was just excited about the bonus time abroad and getting in some much needed exercise.

I can't believe how little I appreciated the Camino at the start, but I quickly came to realize how profound and life-changing the Camino would be in my life. Even on the first day I described an omnipresent feeling of a greater purpose, a feeling which would continue to grow with each person I met and each mile I completed. The Camino evolved and changed me in ways I am still discovering today.

25 mayo, Castrojeriz: "I know that I was drawn to the Camino for the opportunity to see Spain and the amazing natural beauty of its country, but even now, on the second day, I am slowly realizing how much more it is..."

When I was first told of the Camino, I envisioned the Appalachian Trail of the United States' East Coast — miles and miles of wilderness and absolute solitude while traveling in rough, mountainous terrain. Until I arrived at the start of the Camino, I had only visited a brief intersection of that trail which ran close to my college campus in Virginia. With this in the back of my mind, my first thoughts were to find someone to take the risky journey with me, and to learn as much as possible about the trail and the dangers involved. I love the outdoors, but was terrified at the thought of getting lost in the wilderness, let alone in the wilderness of a country of which I had no prior knowledge or experience, and with limited language.

Despite my fears, I neglected to tackle either of my planned preparations until a few weeks before embarking on the almost three-week long adventure. I read a few guides, reviewed numerous publications online and in the local library in Oviedo (where I had been studying for several months beforehand), and even learned about its historical significance in my classes at the university. As it turns out, the Camino is so much more than a cut trail through the wondrous and wild scenery of a beautiful country. It was designed for many travelers on a pilgrimage and it has been traveled and preserved for over a thousand years.

While there are busy seasons on the Camino, which generally follow the traditional work calendar and school holidays, *peregrinos* were always on the trail. The Camino has numerous beginnings that stretch like veins through western Europe. All of these trails converge onto one main path, the Camino Francés, which travels from the border of France straight across the width of northern Spain to the city of Santiago de Compostela, nearly on the opposite coast. I met *peregrinos* who had begun their journey in Belgium, Italy and Germany (each with astonishing stories), but the majority of fellow *peregrinos* I encountered began their journey in St. Jean Pied de Port, or another city along the Camino Francés in Spain.

While studying at the Universidad de Oviedo, I met my traveling companion, an adventuresome and engaging girl from Oregon named Emily. We just happened upon the topic of the Camino one day after classes, and she told me she also planned to walk the path as far as she could in the last days of her stay. We didn't know much else about each other when we met in a bus station to be dropped off in the city of Burgos, just a little more than halfway into the Camino Francés (with 500 kilometers to go), on the 24th of May, 2004. The next morning, Emily and I found an *albergue* to obtain our first stamp that marked our travels in our *Credencial de Peregrino*, and off we went.

29 mayo, Terradillos: "Each pueblo, no matter how small, has the fabulous church or bell tower that we can spot from afar and keep our eye on as a solid goal — they really are a sight for sore eyes and exhausted feet."

Unlike my visions of the wild Appalachian Trail, which runs mostly through a chain of mountain ranges, there were pueblos, towns and cities no more than 10 kilometers apart on the Camino, and each offered a *refugio* or *albergue* with at least the most basic accommodations, all at very little cost. We rarely had to search for shelter or a place to rest. We often slept in places which were awe-inspiring on their own: working monasteries, ancient inns, churches, courtyards, and even private homes. We walked through the smallest towns alongside plots of beautiful gardens, over crumbling Roman bridges, and many times among herds of cows. We walked on dust and dirt that people trod on every day, on fresh manure and pockmarked roads, yet each step was thrilling. I can't describe it any other way; it was the commonness of the path that touched you, and brought so many *peregrinos* to question their place in life, to press on and want to discover more, and to marvel at the beauty in the simple things.

I was especially surprised by the varied terrain on the Camino, which spanned several types of landscapes through the width of the country. We traversed the long, flat plains of the Spanish Meseta with very little shade, to hilly green countryside, steep mountain climbs and thick forests. There were days when fresh mud caked my shoes and walking was slow and careful, and others where we practically ran from one tree to another for a break from the heat. One day we would walk through endless fields of purple and red poppies, and the next would be through a marsh-like trail with tall, prickly grass. We'd enjoy cool breezes from the surrounding valleys, or burning sun on the flat plains. No matter the condition of the day or the ease of the terrain, it was the variety of so many landscapes that was so intriguing and that encouraged us to pause and marvel at our surroundings. I look back on my words today and am immediately taken back to the countryside where the scent of lavender and fragrant flowers swelled in the day's heat. I still remember the smell of wet cobblestones in the morning, soaked with wine or *sidra* (homemade cider) from a gathering the night before, as I walked through the pueblos.

We didn't always tread on carefully worn country paths, however. There were several occasions as we approached larger cities where we were forced to walk directly on the asphalt of a highway. Narrow two-lane roads with cars whizzing by, polluted air, stifling heat without breeze, careless drivers … the path certainly has evolved since the times of monks and monasteries. Even then, when we hated the concrete for being so mercilessly hard and hot, I barely remember a complaint from my fellow travelers. Maybe we just appreciated the quiet walks across endless flatlands and knew there would be more on the other side, or we remembered the back-breaking mountains that we would surely have to climb. But no matter where we were, we were forced to look at our surroundings and take them in. The entire goal of each day was to walk. Walk and *appreciate*. Where else in the world demands so little?

25 mayo, Castrojeriz: 'Silly American girls — you have way too much in your packs!...we should not have made it this far."

6 junio, O Cebreiro: "No make-up, no impressive clothes; nothing even really clean. So simple, so wonderful. And sleep is always welcome whenever you need to, on the side of a hill or in the middle of a field."

On the second day of walking and getting used to our habits, Emily and I discovered we were some of the "slow" ones, completing about 20 kilometers each day. We had to stop almost every hour to rest and relieve our backs, even taking off our tennis shoes and bringing out the flip-flops to relieve our feet. When we arrived at the Convento de San Antón that night we started to moan about our backaches. Upon picking up our packs, a Spanish *peregrino* cursed aloud and said we were crazy to carry so much with us. How dumb we felt. While enjoying a meal of canned tuna and granola, Emily and I stripped our packs to our "bare minimum" and mailed off 10 kilos of excess weight to pick up again in Santiago. Even then we were barely at the level of recommended weight, but as each day went on, we found we needed less and less. In the last days of the Camino, my daily outfit consisted of a tank-top with built-in bra, a thin cotton scarf wrapped around my waist like a skirt, a lightweight rain jacket in case of showers or cool breeze, tennis shoes and the same socks, unwashed, from day one. Everything else was unnecessary, just material wants. From this revelation alone I still keep with me one of the Camino's famous mantras: *"deja lo que puedes, toma lo que necesitas"* — leave what you can, take what you need.

Where we rested our heads at night was never as romantic as the day of walking through open countryside. Sleep became a simple necessity, much like finding a basic *bocadillo* of tough bread and cheese to scrounge up some energy. The *albergues* rarely offered a pillow and, seemed to invite the loudest snorers on the trail, and the ever-present smell of body odor was to be expected. No matter the conditions, we were thankful for the generosity of the church parish, the old hotel or the open floor serving as that night's refuge. Often the cost for a stay was as little as three euros, or even a simple donation of whatever we could spare. I can't thank enough the men and women, all complete strangers, who opened their homes to us. Without a question they led us to a sleeping place and we piled in, too exhausted for words after endless hours of walking. What moves someone to be so gracious and selfless? The question in itself was enough to humble us.

1 junio, León: "[My experience in] Spain has made me realize how much I do not enjoy being alone, for long periods of time, and that I am happiest when I share my time with another person."

"Cuando hablo con otros peregrinos, muchas veces no son españoles y la conversación se convierte en una mezcla de francés, inglés, español, italiano, y cualquier palabra (a veces que no existe en ninguna forma) que podemos decir. Muy gracioso! [When I speak with other pilgrims, many times they are not Spanish and the conversation turns into a mix of French, English, Spanish, Italian and whatever word (which sometimes doesn't even exist) that we can say. Very funny!]

The fact that I do not enjoy being alone for an extended amount of time was of no surprise to me. I began my trip with the need to find a partner, but when Emily had to leave after six days to catch her flight home, a strange thing happened — I no longer feared solitude. I remember it took me a long while to stop looking for where everyone was around me, but I knew that there was no shortage of walking partners on the Camino. I could always run into someone with whom I could keep the pace, share a story, or simply walk beside during the journey. The Camino seemed to offer liberty or community to whoever sought it.

I made many notes in my diary about those I came across: Olivier, the Frenchman who came to the Camino to pray for his two unmarried daughters; the man from Nuremberg who biked from home to benefit a Kiwanis children's charity; Lars, the German fellow whose girlfriend wanted a baby and who needed some time to think; Andreas from Ecuador who took a vacation to travel for religious reasons; Marie Caterine, the 50-something French lady who loved Romanesque churches and had been walking bits of the Camino for 10 years. They came from all corners of the world, mostly single travelers, and each one offered a unique glimpse of humanity.

My only other steady Camino companion after Emily left was a Canadian girl named Kate. She was just a year older than I and had also just finished studying abroad in France. There weren't many young travelers at this stage of the Camino, which is located about a week's walking distance from Santiago, so she was a welcome companion with whom I could connect. We kept passing each other from town to town, but it took a while before we sat together and shared our stories. It seemed to me that she wanted to keep a solitary journey. One night a fellow traveler brought us together over a plate of spaghetti and *serrano* ham, and we immediately began chatting away the late afternoon. Kate had heard of the Camino in Quebec and she knew she wanted to take the opportunity to walk before heading home from her studies. I asked about her motive for taking on the Camino and she thought for a while before quietly stating that her reasons had evolved. On the Camino she found that she could enjoy the little things in life without being blinded by the rush and struggles of home. We could all lead a simple life for a while, appreciating every day, every minute, as our feet took us forward; just follow the yellow arrows. Kate was the first to suggest that I walk alone for an entire day, not comparing myself to other pilgrims and the distance they walked. It was difficult to do, but at the end of the day, I cherished the chance to quietly write in my journal, letting loose all of my thoughts from a day of walking in what, to me, was paradise. I was so grateful to Kate for ultimately pushing me past my comfort zone and helping me learn to wander alone, peacefully, on the Camino.

Those that I remember most were the people I came across in the tiny pueblos, most of which seemed to be nothing more than a tightly packed groups of stone buildings with a communal water fountain in its center. The aged buildings were of the most basic stone design, except for the churches, and many of the towns were so quiet that they seemed abandoned. These were my favorite places because I could see the old man behind a tattered curtain in the window watching the passing *peregrinos*, or the shepherd in the field who would stop herding his sheep to wave hello. No matter what business we *peregrinos* were interrupting as we trudged through the towns, the residents always seemed happy to point us in the right direction or answer a harried question. And despite how exhausted we became, it would make all of our efforts worthwhile when they wished us a "*Buen Camino.*"

One day a fellow *peregrina* and I treated ourselves to the Museo de Chocolate in Astorga, and as we were deciding between the decadent 90% cacao bars, the owner of the museum shop stopped us at the counter. She was your typical elderly Spanish woman, wagging her finger and giving us motherly advice whether we cared for it or not. "Look at that weight you're carrying … and how hot it is outside!" she admonished. We encountered this concern everywhere. Even traveling in large groups we often received advice from the locals and passersby, and they always offered their concerns with care. I will always remember Spain for its people's genuine kindness and hospitality.

As for the company of *peregrinos*, the path that led through Spain was filled with different languages. I recall one particular day walking with Luca, an architect from a small town in northern Italy, along the path from El Burgo Ranero, and we chatted for the length of the 35 kilometers we traversed that day. It was an early start at 5:00 am, and fog covered the uphill path of rough concrete. Despite the difficulty of even breathing as we climbed the steep roads, we shared hours of conversation in a mix of Spanish, Italian and English. God only knows what we talked about — religion, politics, wine — but I remember laughing and smiling during one of the most difficult days on the path. This was just another common, enchanting feature of the Camino.

5 junio, Villafranca del Bierzo: "[I] even completed my personal record so far — 38 kilometers — and spent a night outside in a tent next to the albergue de Molinaseca. Except for the traffic and the mattresses provided, it felt like we were doing the real Camino thing."

Refrán del Camino: "No corras, que a donde tienes que llegar es a ti mismo." [Camino proverb: 'Don't rush, because your destination is your own self."]

It was difficult not to compare my pace with that of my fellow *peregrinos*, or to be caught in a long conversation and end up walking for much longer than intended. I had no real itinerary or deadline for the Camino, but as we got closer, there were many who did. There was the *dominguero* (Sunday stroller), or the *mínimo peregrino*, the leisurely walkers or tourists who would only complete the minimum 100 kilometers to receive the pilgrim's *Compostela*. Crowds grew as we approached Santiago, and it became ever harder to find the quiet nights in smaller *albergues*. I tried to leave earlier and earlier in the morning because the *refugios* would fill up in the early afternoon and I'd be forced to walk to another town, or sleep outdoors. The one occasion when I "roughed it" in a tent was still rewarding, and my companions reflected on how the real *peregrinos* of ages past went through much worse. We were fortunate to be given the luxuries we could find and that were given freely to us.

In the last few days I came across more English speakers — church and student groups who walked in droves for the last five days — and I immediately distanced myself from them. I didn't look like an American anymore, rather more like a ragged, sweaty nomad, and I didn't speak up when they were around. In my head, however, I wanted to share with them the meaning of the Camino and what I had experienced. I wanted to tell them to stop running towards Santiago, to appreciate each step. They angered me with their buses and their travel guides walking alongside, but it disappointed me that I became so bitter towards them. I traveled in more silence in those last days, so as not to be discovered or associated with the tourists. I stopped more, and made the excuse to write more in my diary just to try to capture as much as I could before it was all over.

10 junio, Santa Irene: "Caña con limón in hand, yellow canaries in cages singing individual concerts, tired muscles and eye lids, seeking shade under an Estrella Galicia bar umbrella...only 70 kilometers away from our goal and yet we are so hesitant to reach it."

11 junio, somewhere outside of Lavacolla: "I found a quiet spot where I can hear the flowing water of a nearby stream ... my back is against a broken piece of wall, and though I can hear almost everyone who passes about 50 m away, I'm glad to have found tranquility and rest."

12 junio, Santiago de Compostela: "I enjoyed going through the rituals because pilgrims had done the same for centuries before me, but I wish in some way I didn't feel so rushed by the masses of tourists and could truly appreciate the sacredness at the end of the pilgrimage ... Compostelas in hand, we proudly heard the list of peregrinos that arrived that day (from Burgos, an American!)."

The last day before coming into Santiago, my companions and I split up to enjoy the Camino as it was meant to be enjoyed — alone and in reflection. When I read my words now, there was such a struggle with my desire to stay in the place I had come to love, and to reach a goal we had expended such effort to meet.

As I descended into the city of Santiago, my feet fell slow and heavily as I neared the finish. I could see the gothic spires of the Cathedral from my last *refugio*, an ancient building with tall ceilings and long, open corridors where hundreds of cots were placed side by side, almost like a military hospital ward. It was situated on a hill overlooking the city, and I remember fighting myself with the decision of staying in this very crowded refuge and continuing my time on the Camino for as long as I could stand, or buckling down and running to the finish line. In the end, I just stayed an extra afternoon to write in my journal and made plans to be one of the first *peregrinos* to seek my *Compostela* first thing in the morning.

It was a Saturday when I stepped across the wide public square at the rear of the Cathedral and walked into a corridor along the back of the church. The passageway took the line of *peregrinos* above a sacred space where the supposed remains of St. James lay below our feet, and I took a brief moment to realize that I had officially reached my goal, and the goal of millions of *peregrinos* before me. We then circled around to the front of the cathedral and had to step back several yards to take in the view of the majestic architecture. The sight was truly breath-taking. A fellow *peregrino* took my camera and captured the moment that I dropped my heavy pack and threw my hands up high as I stood at its entrance. I had made it.

I experienced a whirlwind of emotions in those last hours in the city before my bus to Madrid departed, a mixture of excitement and accomplishment, but also dread at returning to the world I knew before. Away from the Saturday afternoon crowd in the city and the groups of celebrating *peregrinos*, I felt I needed to be alone. Curled up in a café chair and with my last *caña con limón*, I passed the time sketching examples of the beautiful architecture and trying to gather my thoughts and reflections on the journey. I mentioned more than once in my diary that this should not be my only trip on the Camino. As I often remark to those who talk about their travels abroad, a piece of my heart most assuredly remains in Spain, and I have hope that I will be able to return and reignite the passion in these diary pages.

> *29 mayo, Terradillos: "He told me to be careful in asking the question. The Camino, he said, is something private, individual, and clearly not something that everyone understands or will understand until maybe even 10 years later."*

> *13 junio, leaving Santiago: "You could see it in our eyes when we talked about the Camino, when we shared reflections and emotions ... also the fear of cheating ourselves, of forgetting the one place in our hearts we finally discovered."*

A few months after returning to the States, I was daydreaming while working online and tried a basic search on the Camino de Santiago. After perusing a few pictures at different stages of the Camino, it pained me to see several sites dedicated to making the trip more convenient — "Group Packages," "Day Tours," "Prearranged Accommodations." To the unfamiliar, it appears at first glance to be an easy hiking trip for the nature lover, or a quick religious experience for the believer, but then I remembered my own initial reasons for embarking on the Camino: for school credit and good exercise. I was no better. I had no idea what to expect when I began my journey, and I still can't describe the distinctive shift in my view on life with which I concluded it.

The only way I can describe the Camino's effect on my life is in the way the Camino opened up to me, the way it allowed me to think beyond the simple matters of worldly necessities and material gains, and the way in which it remains in my heart. I can confidently say that I grew as a person during the 18 days I traveled on foot with 10 kilos of nothing but the bare minimum on my back, consuming only enough food for energy and sustenance, and viewing humanity through a new and open lens. I grew stronger, more reflective, more humble, more self-aware, and more appreciative than when I began as an adventure-seeking college student. Perhaps the most universal truth that any *peregrino* can share is that the Camino does not stop at the Cathedral. It has not left me, and for that I am forever grateful.

GROWING UP

Daniel W. Hieber

18 GOING ON 19

My nineteenth birthday was still thirty-two days away when I started the descent from Roncesvalles. Thirty-two days, I would discover, was more than just a month. It was a lifetime. It was looking back on everything I had accomplished, and all I had yet to do. Somewhere between 18 and 19, I had gained a year's worth of meditation and experience.

It began that first day on the trail from Roncesvalles. Those first few days are still the clearest in my mind. Everything, both life and landscape, had a glorious feeling of freshness to it. I remember celebrating that first twenty-seven kilometer trek with a plunge into the river at Larrasoaña at day's end. The mountain stream was icy cold — it had probably been snow twenty minutes before — but we didn't care. We were invincible! We were tired and hungry and still far outside any established comfort zone, but the sheer...fullness...of that first day swept all that away. The showers later were even colder than the river, but we laughed it off, soaking up the experience.

Just before Puente la Reina we took an unexpected detour and crossed onto the Camino Aragonés, arriving at a little place called Eunate. It was like something in a children's fable. At the end of a long dirt road was a little church surrounded by fields of swaying wheat, cared for by a smiling woman named Mariluz who lives in the railroad-style flat nearby. She took us into her home that night, and made it *our* home too. We ate well that day. It is one of the amazing feats of the pilgrims that, out of the varying scraps tucked away at the bottom of packs, they can, when the need arises, produce a feast by any meaning of the term. It never failed to amaze me the entire trip, and especially that day in Eunate, what the pilgrims were capable of producing *together*, every one putting in their share. Later that night, Mariluz prepared us the best dinner we had our entire time in Spain. Since we were starving from our daily exertion, anything we ate took on the sweet savor of success for a long day.

After dinner we slipped out into the night, proceeding by candlelight to the little church. We settled in, intrigued. Mariluz, seated ceremoniously before the altar, began to sing. I knew not the words that came from her lips — I could only recognize it as Latin — but her voice resounded off the stone walls, filling that tiny space with its exquisite hum. I drifted off to sleep that night to the sweet memory of that beautiful hymn.

The next days passed quickly — a lifetime in a single moment. Puente la Reina came and went. We all walked the same road now. The crisp beauty of the cathedral at Nájera, with its crystal flowers dotting the cloister, passed through my life in mere hours. I was lost in Logroño and found again before I knew it.

But the first time I consciously tasted the real meaning of the Camino was Tosantos, nine days out from Roncesvalles. It was there I met José Luís. He, like Mariluz, had dedicated himself to the Camino and what it represents. He held an evening service for the pilgrims in the tiny chapel of his *albergue*. After singing *Ultreia* for the dozenth time, the pilgrims dispersed. José Luís, I think, was better at philosophizing than preaching. Luckily for me, I got to hear him do both.

I caught him in the kitchen after dinner. I wanted to hear what he had to say about the Camino. I was not disappointed. He was a "Camino philosopher." We talked over tea deep into the night. The next day found my mind racing. The Camino begins in you, and ends in God, he said. It never really ends, but becomes a way to live by. What did that *mean*? How could the Camino become a way of life? I thought long and hard on these questions for the next weeks. Slowly, the answers would dawn on me, but it was a gradual, grinding process. Eventually, it would reshape my entire schema of the world.

I continued on. I walked across the Meseta and into mountainous Galicia. I left my stone at the base of the *Cruz de Ferro*. I walked on.

O Cebreiro is scary for any pilgrim. It's high. It was a little scarier for me, because just before the *Cruz de Ferro*, my trusty staff had been stolen. Now I faced O Cebreiro, my first climb without it. I didn't know what to expect. I was mad at myself for forming a dependency to begin with. O Cebreiro was a *hard* day. Lesson learned. The staff was just an object, like any other.

I reached the top of the mountain late that day. I rested twice, which only made me less inclined to continue. But as I finally topped the rise, my weariness melted away. The hills I had just climbed sat glorious under the afternoon sun, and I was on top of it all, looking down on God's great creation. If Spain is a place of beauty, the overlook from O Cebreiro is a place of the gods. In that moment, the day's hike seemed infinitesimally unimportant compared to how good I felt right then.

I arrived at Santiago a week or so later, filled with memories. Each day had had its own lesson, something that would stay with me forever. As I sat there reflecting on the cathedral's beauty, a strange feeling came over me. Suddenly I was remembering the river at Larrasoaña, imagining the feeling of triumph at the top of O Cebreiro, reliving the memories of that little church at Eunate. My journey was complete. Now it was time to return to that other journey called life, and the memories it had in store.

FIVE YEARS LATER

A good friend taught me the importance of outgrowing things in life. I remember chattering away at him one day, swelling with pride at having mastered the tricks of the "real world," telling him how I had finally lost my crazy college sleep schedule, how much I enjoyed having a place of my own to take care of, and how mature I had become in my work habits. My friend, who is a good deal my elder, replied with a knowing smile, "See? You've outgrown this whole college thing. You've moved on to bigger and better things!"

I admit I bridled at first. Admitting that you've been young and naïve in the past is always embarrassing, especially when somebody else recognizes it before you do and is patiently waiting for you to realize it too. But maybe that embarrassment is just pride on my part, and one day I'll learn to outgrow that as well. Whatever the case, my friend is a wise man, and his words stuck with me.

Outgrowing things is important if we are to have any aspirations in life. I've seen too many of my friends who have yet to outgrow college, for example. They continue to haunt their old college hangouts, to cheer at the same ritual football games every weekend, and to have the same crazy parties afterwards. I wonder if they'll ever snap out of it.

We outgrow our relationships, too, sadly. When we're lucky, our friends grow with us, and we learn to remake our relationships as an adult. Former professors become friends, mentors become colleagues, and parents become partners. Sharing fun experiences as college buddies now becomes sharing sobering experiences as adults. We grow up together.

The trick is learning to let go, and if there's one thing the Camino is good at, it's that. You let go of your comforts, your work, your iPod, and your doubts. You plan like hell until you take that first step on the trail, and then you learn to let go of the need to be in complete control, and start to trust in the kindness of strangers. Learning to let go of the trivial and the meaningless is one of the most important lessons the Camino teaches. What pilgrim hasn't returned from his journey, walked into his home, and said, "Look at all this junk!" Learning to let go of all that *stuff* helps recapture the sense of freedom that comes from realizing that all you need is a pack and a warm place to sleep at night. It makes you value the things you do keep that much more. The Camino teaches us this art of letting go — it teaches us to be *free*.

If I sound like an Eastern ascetic monk at this point, it should come as no surprise. Taoism, for example, literally translates as "path" or "way," just as does *camino*. In some ways the Camino isn't particularly unique — any true journey (i.e. any pilgrimage) ought to teach the same things. Metaphors abound on such journeys, but the fundamental characteristic of any pilgrimage is that it is a physical journey that represents a non-physical goal. The point of the pilgrimage is to transcend the physical in search of the spiritual, emotional, or philosophical. Fundamental to this process is the act of letting go. We cannot find the spiritual if we are fixated on the physical; yet paradoxically, it is the physical act of pilgrimage which sets us on our path to wisdom. And so the Camino is just one of many paths to wisdom, one particular set of yellow arrows pointing towards truth, God, or serenity. With this realization, I have outgrown the Camino.

During my four years in college, I completed no fewer than three Caminos. And since we're already talking about being embarrassingly naïve, I'll tell you my original reason for doing the Camino: I wanted to be different. I wanted to have an *experience*, not your typical study abroad to Europe. Intuitively and subconsciously I understood that with this different experience would come a different and more valuable perspective than if I had done a typical study abroad. At the moment, I just wanted to do something exciting.

Thankfully, I've outgrown that phase of my life. It's fortunate too that my desire to stand out from the pack would provide me with an experience that had meaningful and instructive effects on my life. I could have been a career bungee-jumper, but for all its exoticness, I doubt I would have learned much from the experience. I no longer have the same reasons that I once did for doing the Camino. I've outgrown them and let them go. I have transcended the experience of the Camino for the broader experience of pilgrimage. What's great about pilgrimages is that they change as we do — our reasons for doing them and the lessons we take from them only get richer as we become wiser. Like old friends that have stuck with us, our pilgrimages mature as we do.

What's most surprising to me when I reread the article I wrote five years ago is not how naïve I was, but rather, how much I had already learned to let go. José Luis's philosophy that "the Camino begins in you and ends in God" had nothing to do with Santiago de Compostela, and everything to do with taking the most meaningful pieces of the Camino with you and leaving the rest behind. He taught me that the Camino is just one experience, one tradition, but that we can transcend it by taking the lessons from it and incorporating them into a way of life. After all, what is the point of a pilgrimage if we can never learn to leave it behind and return, wiser, to our lives?

And so I had already begun to learn the wisdom in letting go when I wrote, "My journey was complete. Now it was time to return to that other journey called life." Yet secretly I hope that one day, my path will take me back to the Camino, because while individual Caminos are something we outgrow, our pilgrimages will always grow with us.

MY BROKEN ROAD TO SANTIAGO

Allison Gray

I was 19 years old in June 2001. I had little clue where life would take me and admittedly very little direction. There was, in fact, only one thing that I knew I wanted to do with my life. Only a few days prior I had returned from Spain, where I completed the Camino for the first time as a student with a Roanoke College group. As I walked into my office building for my summer job a week later, I told myself that if I did nothing else, I would return to the Camino at least once more. I am not sure why I felt so strongly about returning; all I knew was that there was something still in Santiago that I needed to go back for.

Two years went by. I finished college and was interviewing for my first full-time job. I told my interviewer, who would be my boss when I was hired, that I would not accept the job if she could not promise me a month of unpaid leave at some undetermined time in the future. Thankfully, she required only a six-month-notice and a promise to train the person who would fill in for me while I was gone. Two more years went by and I woke up one morning and knew that the time had come to give that six-month-notice. Having to give a six-month-notice was fortunate because I needed that time to prepare after making a spur-of-the-moment decision.

My preparations were intense; I had two huge mountains to scale even before departing for the Pyrenees. First was obviously physical shape. I worked out four hours a day with a personal trainer five days a week and on Sundays I would go hiking after church, carrying a full pack and wearing my boots.

The second was the harder mountain by far: I had to mentally prepare. I have suffered from anorexia and have been about thirty pounds underweight since I was fifteen. My doctor told me I had to gain twenty pounds before she would approve my leaving. Those pounds would prove to be important for carrying my gear as well; I had already cinched the hip-band on my pack as small as it could go. If I lost any weight then the hip band would not fit at all, and I would not be able to wear the pack properly. Also, I had been diagnosed with bi-polar depression and was on a new, dangerous drug. It was possible that, while I was in Spain, I could develop a fatal reaction to this medication, so I had to choose between finally being *normal* or returning to my usual battle to appear okay without having any nearby support system on which to rely. I eventually gained nineteen pounds and left with my medication but without my doctor's approval.

My road to Santiago was much longer than 500 miles; it was six months of retraining and teaching myself to actually live instead of survive. Survival would come back into play very quickly though. On a muddy day about six or seven days in, I fractured my foot. The amazing thing about fractures is how easy they are to ignore. Six days later I was still walking decently, and had convinced myself that I had a slight case of tendonitis in the other foot. My first lesson for the Camino: I could do anything — including complete my journey — as long as I had that tub of anti-inflammatory cream. My second lesson was that no matter how carefully you walk, you cannot fool a fellow pilgrim into thinking you are not in pain. It was through these two lessons that I learned my first Camino-related life lesson: although you set out alone, there is no reason to always remain that way.

Friends are made quickly, creating deep, personal, whirlwind connections that last a few days before a difference in pace separates you. I was lucky to come across many true, instant friends. An Italian man tried to show me how to go slow (even though Americans are mostly incapable of going slow). There were five minutes under some apple trees where I *almost* understood. For the record, I was sad to walk away from

86

him when he wanted to take a nap, but you just never know if there is going to be room in the *albergue*. I met a German man who walked away from me when he decided that my injuries were too severe to continue; I was pleased to see his face and show him he was wrong when I passed him on the Camino. I met a group of Italian pilgrims on horseback who welcomed me so warmly into their group that I completely trusted them, and when they offered me the sucker part of an octopus tentacle, I ate it. I like to think that they still think of my reaction, and laugh. I met a Canadian girl so free-spirited that I still have doubts that she has ever found her way back to her family and job in Canada. In my head, she has not, and that makes me smile. She planted in my head the idea that walking the last leg of the Camino overnight was the *only* way to walk into Santiago.

Finally, there was an American. It was he who gave me strength when I had none. This American had left his job in a similar manner as I had, so we shared that early on. He also had leg problems, and I shared my cream. He went with me when I finally went to the doctor who upheld my diagnosis of tendonitis (because I finally had developed it in the unbroken foot) and told me to stop. He walked slower with me, because I could not walk fast anymore. He said he was inspired by me, that he could finish each day because I could finish each day, and I was surely in more pain than he was. I told him that it was simply a matter of putting one foot in front of the other — it was my mantra — and I could not fathom being in too much pain to move one foot one step ahead. So he walked with me and pushed me to achieve our daily goal, until we were two days out. Those two days were the culmination of everything I had wanted and not wanted for my journey, and were the most important days of my trip.

The morning started out like any other; breakfast was small and early with the sun just starting to rise as we set out. It was going to be a long day. By my guidebook, we were still three days away from Santiago, but *we* were confident that we could make it in two. I could envision my Italian friend shaking his head sadly at this thought. It was do-able though, so I thought.

I was very wrong. We could not have been more than 50 meters out of town before my month-long mantra failed me. I was less than 75 kilometers away from Santiago, and I could not imagine putting one foot in front of the other one more time. Trying to hide my utter despair, I returned to the bar while my friend consoled me. There, he gave me his walking sticks, which I needed to walk, and he took my Leatherman Micra multi-tool, which he was quite fond of, to hold onto until I returned his sticks to him. We parted with the agreement that we would meet again at 11:00 the next day in front of the cathedral to trade back. He left, believing that I would get on a bus and stay in a hotel in Santiago until he could get there. This is not what happened.

I tell myself that I *tried* to listen when the bartender directed me to the bus station and told me when the next bus left. That is why I had him tell me three times. In reality, I don't know why I could not make sense of his words and did not recall any of them when I walked out the door a few minutes later. "Stubborn" is probably somewhere in the reason. Instead of finding a bus, I found a van. Here entered the Italian pilgrims on horseback. Through an exchange that capitalized on their limited English and familiarity with Spanish, I told them my story of how I came to be on the side of the road that morning. They discussed my situation and decided that if I traveled with them, riding with their ferriers, then I would not be breaking my pilgrimage and could still get my stamps for the *Compostela*. I was upset by the thought of riding in their van, but they consoled me by saying that the original pilgrims would have done whatever was necessary to get to Santiago, and it was fine for me to do the same. They would arrive in Santiago on the day after next, putting me one day behind my friend but maintaining my pilgrim status, so I chose to go with them. Excluding the octopus, it was an uneventful day, which ended in them dropping me off at the *albergue* with plans to pick me up later for dinner. Again, this is not what happened.

The *albergue* was completely full, so I was told to go down to the hotel. I had the money and could easily get to the hotel and back before the Italians picked me up, but I had no desire to stay there. I quickly came to a crossroads: either turn right and go to the hotel, or turn left and continue walking the few remaining kilometers and reach the goal of arriving in Santiago by 11 a.m. the next day. This gave me 18 hours to complete my journey, a distance which would have taken five or six hours at the beginning of the month, but one that I did not know if I could complete now. After a quick stop at the store to buy yogurt, a bar of chocolate, and some new batteries for my now-dead flashlight, I chose to continue walking. I never saw my Italian friends again.

I had heard that Santiago was absolutely beautiful when seen from high in the hills under a rising sun. What I hadn't heard was how scary that last leg of the way could be. I was raised in a city and I knew people who had been attacked by strangers hiding behind trees, so walking through a serene forest landscape was far from peaceful once the sun went down. As I said previously, this was the culmination of my five-year-long journey to return to Santiago. I was unsure that I could accomplish my task and I was all alone, with no one who truly believed that I could do what I was doing. I didn't even know whether I could make it, but my feet held up as long as I repeatedly told myself to keep putting one foot in front of the other. I kept up an agonizingly slow pace for the first few hours, but I eventually fell into rhythm with my MP3 player, and moved a bit faster. Then it dawned on me: I had been thinking about doing this midnight walk for weeks and now I was hiding behind an audio book so that I could be spared the fright of my situation. I stopped for a snack and put my MP3 player away, and took a few minutes to think of the time that I heard the idea of a midnight walk into Santiago.

It was about two weeks prior, I was still walking with the German, and we had stopped in a restaurant for a bite to eat and got to talking with a Canadian who was working there. She told us how she was wandering around Europe and heard about the Camino, so she decided to do it. She had already completed her Camino and was simply wandering wherever she could find short-term employment. She had walked into Santiago at sunrise and when she told us of it, the beauty of what she had seen was reflected in her face, and I knew that I wanted to have a memory like that of my own.

Without my MP3 player running, I was able to soak in the beauty of my surroundings. I felt so brave! I had not been too afraid to ask for leave from my job. I had not been too afraid to spend most of my savings to come to Spain a second time. I had not been too afraid to come to Spain alone. I would not be too afraid to enjoy my walk! I had been so afraid of so many things, but this was my chance to be fearless, and I seized it. I saw the Camino at every hour of the day. I started walking at four-thirty that evening and at six o'clock the next morning I was there! I ate the last of my snack overlooking the hills at Santiago, watching the sun rise. I had been told that there was nothing as beautiful as this, and I agree wholeheartedly. Many details of my two trips have faded from my mind, but the first views of Santiago are and were unforgettable, and there is no explaining what happens when combining this first glimpse of Santiago with the wonder and awe of the sunrise.

I was still walking at eleven, trying to get to the cathedral. I was twenty minutes late meeting my friend, but he was there. I was completely overwhelmed by walking into the cathedral and seeing its splendor and my friend just inside the door. I had accomplished everything that I had set out to do. I did all on my own, but I was never actually alone. Walking the Camino for the first time showed me what I was capable of doing, but the second time allowed me to prove myself. I have grown into a stronger, more driven person, capable of doing anything that I set my mind to. I have been able to achieve everything that I have set my mind to since returning from the Camino, and I believe I have St. James to thank for this.

ROUTINE, SIMPLICITY, AND FOOT FIRST AID:

THE CAMINO DE SANTIAGO

Drew A. Cumings-Peterson

When people ask me about my tattoo, I start by telling them that I spent a month during the summer of 2006 walking from St. Jean Pied de Port, France, across northern Spain. (It's also on my résumé and it kills in interviews.) I explain that the Camino has existed since the Middle Ages; that "El Camino de Santiago" means "The Way of St. James;" and that the Camino ends at the city called Santiago de Compostela, where the bones of St. James allegedly rest. I let them know that my tattoo is a symbol that pilgrims see all over the Camino; that the scallop shell is a symbol of St. James and that it — along with a yellow arrow — is one of the signs that points you in the correct direction on the path. I tell them that I went alone and that three of the friends that I met on the Camino also have the same tattoo.

People respond to this in a variety of ways. Some ask me about the religious experience; some nod knowingly, saying things like "What an opportunity!" or "That must have been some trip." Most people smile politely and ask how much it hurt to get a tattoo on the top of my foot. I smile and tell them the Camino hurt my feet much more than the tattoo. I add that some of the other pilgrims and I had a joke for when our feet hurt — because of the blisters and the calluses — "No Spain Without Pain." That's generally the extent of the introduction to my month-long pilgrimage, but there's more to the story.

I'm not religious but it's hard to explain my experience on the Camino without sounding spiritual. Somewhere in week two or three, while walking through the pain, it occurred to me that a normal person is lucky to feel alive in the fullest sense maybe a few times a year. Alive in the way you don't forget. Alive in the way that months and years later, you can remember the taste of the air you were breathing or the smell of the food you were eating. A few instances of this every year might be normal, but I felt that alive every day on the Camino.

The daily memories are just as vivid to me as if I had finished the Camino yesterday. I remember walking the first day and meeting a group of old French women who were in much better shape than I was (at 19 years old) — who taught me to say my feet hurt: *J'ai mal au pied*. That was also the day I ran out of water and was too proud to ask the other pilgrims for help; when I finally got to *The Fountain of Roland* — the first of many fountains, I was so thankful for a drink that I named my walking stick "Roland." I remember the first time I ate dinner with a woman on hiatus from her job in San Francisco and two Canadian international-tour-guides-to-the-elderly who would become my best friends from the trip — the four of us all have the same tattoo. I remember a dinner during the World Cup where I counted all the pilgrims in the room to find we represented fourteen different countries. Then there was the day I was standing outside a church in a small town along the path and a flock of birds flew over head and all decided to go to the bathroom while flying over me (thank God, I wore a hat). I also remember, over the course of the Camino, realizing how perfect it was to see so many modern windmills in the land of Cervantes. Also, climbing a steep hill in western Spain and feeling, for the first time, a sense of completeness that I can only relate to descriptions I've read of *nirvana* — not wanting anything, not needing anything, no feeling the pain in my feet; serenity. From the span of my short life, the memories from the Camino are the most vivid, complete, and calming memories and they come from a single month.

The frustrating part of explaining my time on the Camino (and the reason I don't really try to explain it to non-pilgrims) is convincing other people that the power of the trip boils down to a routine of perseverance and simplicity. I woke up every morning with the thirty or forty people I came to know so well; we ate bread and coffee, helped each other take care of the foot first aid, walked for a few hours, stopped at a restaurant where we took off our shoes and re-did our foot first aid while eating, walked for a while longer, stopped at the *albergues* for the night, where we showered, ate, and got ready for the next day by re-doing our foot first aid before bed. We did that every day for a month, and it was the most calming month I've ever had. Along the way, we witnessed beautiful terrain and had stimulating conversations, but what made it so peaceful was that the routine framed it. I remember so much of my experience because I wasn't trying to make a memory out of it; it all just happened while I was walking.

An important part of the routine was what it wasn't. The Camino's focal point is not making memories, remembering your keys, returning calls to your friends, email, going to the movies, or figuring out what clothes to wear. Those things can all happen on the Camino, but they are never the basis for the pilgrimage. The basis is waking up, fixing your feet, and walking to the next stop. The next day, you wake up, fix your feet, and walk to the next stop. The rest is details. The people are transient — some stopped their pilgrimage before I did but others started in their place. I never had *my* computer to keep track of or even *my* first-aid materials to watch out for. Pilgrims share pretty much everything with each other, which means that each pilgrim does what s/he can to keep going and also helps the others get as far as they feel like they need to go. I didn't even need to talk with my fellow pilgrims, except to say *Buen Camino*; there was an old Japanese man and a couple of Italians whom I am sure I knew very well merely by having walked and eaten with them every day for a month, but we never said more to one another than *Buen Camino*. The routine requires nothing more than to make the decision each morning to go as far as you would like. Because everything else amounted to frivolous details, the details were captivating. Since I didn't place emotional baggage on them (like I normally do), I could enjoy them.

This is a difficult lesson to take back to the land of cars, books, Facebook, work, family, friends, bachelor parties, and other things that get in the way of the routine. These things are not evil; they're delightful. But they are only delightful when I ditch the baggage and frame them correctly, the way the Camino made me frame them.

Since I finished, I've tried several things to retain the Camino's message. For a while, I made a rule where I had to give away two things a day. They could be simple things such as a book and a CD, or a chair and a frisbee. I did this for a few months and it was a good exercise; it reflected the aspect of the Camino that reminded me that my focus should just be to keep going and let the other things come and go, so that I could really enjoy them. I also tried to exercise more; I took to running three to four times a week for two years after I finished the Camino (I've learned I like walking more than I like running). I even tried joining Facebook groups dedicated to the Camino to try and connect with people who have gone the Way of St. James, but none of it added up to keeping the Camino in my life, day to day.

Recently, I've decided to stop trying to do anything. I wasn't trying on the Camino. I just kept going. This decision has been the best step I've taken toward keeping the Camino's lessons in my day-to-day life.

Only two times since I finished the Camino have I run into someone who has walked the Way of St. James, and both times I felt like I was meeting family. The first time, I was riding on a bus in Spain, a couple of weeks after finishing my pilgrimage, when a woman saw my tattoo and asked me when I had done the Camino. Other people in Spain knew about el Camino de Santiago, (kind of in the way Americans who haven't seen it know of the majesty of the Grand Canyon) but I could tell by the way she asked that she had been a pilgrim herself. When I told her I had only finished a few weeks before, she pointed toward the ground and asked me how my feet were healing. How I had missed people asking me about the health of my feet! The second time I met someone who had walked on the Camino was several months later, at a coffee shop in Iowa City.

Similarly to my first experience, a woman in line saw my tattoo and asked me if I had done the Camino. We talked briefly, but it felt so good to talk to someone who understood what the tattoo meant.

My tattoo reminds me of the Camino's lessons and it's on my foot for a good reason. After a month of pain and learning foot first aid, the tattoo had to be there. And the lesson remains, though I forget sometimes. Usually, at my most stressed out, I get home at the end of the day and see my foot when I take off my shoes and socks (four years later and I still think the best way to relax is to give my feet air, something I never did before the Camino). After a break, I go for a walk. Some people walk to take a break, but for me, after the Camino, the walk is my internal signal that I'm keeping going; that the stress is probably related to something about which I shouldn't be stressing the details.

I worry that this message is a little trite. "Keep going, keep it simple." I would agree except this is what I took from the Camino. It took me a month and hundreds of dollars in first aid gear, but I think I'm lucky for having received the lesson that so many of my friends don't understand.

I'm lucky because, whereas so many people have heard the message of perseverance and simplicity without experiencing it, I went to Spain with basically nothing in my backpack but a change of clothes, a sweater, a sleeping bag, a journal, my walking stick, my hat, a flashlight, my passport, a toothbrush, a pack towel, shoes, sandals, and my debit card. Everything else, I picked up as I needed along the way. If I can live for a month like that, I can live forever (though I'd have to make money somehow). Anything more than these things on the Camino is dead weight. We don't have to travel so lightly in our day-to-day lives, but the Camino taught me that there is a lot weighing me down that won't if I don't let it.

Buen Camino.

WALKING WITH THE WORLD

Paul Oliver

The best way to visualize the Camino de Santiago is to look at a globe. Put a finger on the border of France and Spain, about halfway between the Atlantic Ocean and the Mediterranean Sea. Put another finger on the northwest corner of Spain, just above Portugal. The imaginary line connecting these two points is the Camino de Santiago. For me, measuring the Camino this way, rather than with numbers, is the best way to measure the centuries-old pilgrimage route that I hiked in the summer of 2006. Measuring with relative distances to the world in which we live puts the accomplishment in perspective. Not many people can say they've hiked a distance visible on a globe.

But there's another reason I look at the globe. It reveals the origins of all the hikers who undertake the Camino de Santiago. People from almost every country representing all six inhabited continents have at some point hiked this very route. That's a lot of people from many corners of the world hiking along the same narrow path toward Santiago de Compostela. Together we have walked the same miles, shared the same carb-loaded dinners, and rested our weary, blistered feet in the same Spanish *albergues*. The Camino does create a rare, if not unique, international community, bound by the same goal, in the same place, at the same time.

There are many reasons people hike the Camino: religion, history, tourism, adventure, curiosity. I came for a little bit of all of this, but under different circumstances than most *peregrinos*.

I was one of 13 people — 11 students and 2 Spanish instructors — participating in a summer study abroad program for undergraduates at the University of Michigan. The program offered a diverse range of field sites and research topics, from international business studies in China to healthcare in Hungary to an exploration of modern Vietnam. I felt overwhelmed with good options as I scanned the list before me, imagining what I might see or do. But one program grabbed my attention more than the others: an ambitious 500-mile trek across northern Spain from the rarefied air of the Pyrenees to the medieval city of Santiago de Compostela. After a long consideration of my options and a conversation with the group's leaders, I signed up. I was on my way.

Looking back after four years, I think I understand the program better. More specifically, I understand the title, "Creating an Inclusive Community on the Way: Adventure Education for the New Millennium." To be honest, I did not lend much thought to the meaning of the title at the time. Yes, I understood the general concept of the mobile community, but my understanding of what the leaders had in mind was vague at best. I was certainly unable to *internalize* the meaning. In the summer of 2006, I was more interested in merely completing the hike. With a combination of diligence and fear, I unpacked my boots, stuffed my new backpack with books, and completed all of the recommended miles of training. The back roads of my home town were transformed into the dirt path of the Camino. The July corn harvest mimicked the pastoral vineyards of Rioja. And my Spanish audiotapes reinforced my modest Spanish vocabulary. But this was no Camino. I was alone. The goal of the program was community, and there is no replacement for that on the lonely back roads of rural Michigan.

The concept of community has been radically transformed in the past few years. The new wave of social networking is changing how humans interact with each other faster than we are able to comprehend the consequences. To put things in perspective, when I hiked the Camino in 2006 as a 19-year-old undergraduate student, Facebook was really hot stuff. This was back in the day when an ".edu" email address was a prerequisite for membership, and even then only a small handful of colleges and universities was among "the chosen." I could go home and brag about my Facebook account in front of jealous high schoolers or even other college students left off the list. 2006 was long before our parents and grandparents had joined, in effect ruining the website's last vestiges of prestige. Facebook's legal battles, privacy wars, and blockbuster movie were absent. Twitter had yet to be invented. Even for an IT analyst like me, the pace of technological development is stunning. Our society cannot seem to find satisfaction with our current means of communication, so we continue to seek more information, from more people, in more mediums — and do it all faster.

In this context the Camino transported us to a different time period. Our group was largely removed from the constant, unyielding communication of the internet age. We didn't have cell phones, for example. Yes, computer access was frequently available at *albergues*, but we used it sparingly. Some small villages didn't even provide the option. The group maintained a blog which we used to keep track of our progress, but sporadic entries resulted in a rather truncated image of our travels.

There are many long hikes out there and more than enough outdoor opportunities (the Appalachian Trail comes to mind.) But the Camino is an interesting fusion of modernity and tradition. It's a blend of outdoor adventure — the Pyrenean climb from St. Jean Pied de Port, France, to Roncesvalles, Spain, for example — and modern urbanism — Pamplona, Burgos, León, and Santiago de Compostela. One hikes through the countryside, but does not camp. One enjoys the convenience of a hot meal and a cold beer, but does so while wearing sweaty clothes that haven't been washed properly in three weeks. One can sit in air-conditioned comfort, sipping a *café con leche*, but only after hiking 15 miles in 95-degree heat.

I recently heard an NPR story about the proliferation of internet connectivity at U.S. campgrounds. According to the report, over 75% of private campgrounds in the United States have Wi-Fi connectivity. Even the National Parks are adding Wi-Fi to visitors' centers. And unless you are reading this essay on a laptop on the beach, you'll recognize the irony.

It's hard to escape the modern age, even when we flee to the countryside. When I heard this story, I instantly thought my trek across Spain. What would the journalist say about the Camino? Is it too connected to the outside world? Is the internet ruining the experience? Are we improving our quality of life or fooling ourselves into isolation?

There's a lot of real face time in the Camino's 480 miles. Hiking for 32 days leaves hours and hours for thinking and talking — with real people no less — from all over the world. For the so-called Facebook Generation, it all seems rather anachronistic. But the benefit of this slowing down of life manifests itself in the development of human relationships that I still remember fondly to this day. Without a doubt, my most memorable experiences were the people I met along the way: the Hungarians, Brits, Germans, Brazilians, and of course, Spaniards. Some of the *albergues* posted world maps with pins representing the home towns of all the people who had passed through their doors. The project turned a two-dimensional map into a three-dimensional mountain range stretching across the world.

There were so many people from countless countries, each with a good story to tell. I met an iconoclastic, *mate*-sipping Canadian who worked at the front office of the Puente de Órbigo *albergue*. His hippie style, *mate* tea addiction, and easy conversation made him instantly likeable. On another stage of the hike, I ran into a German man who was taking time off between jobs. We walked together for a while and shared a bit about our lives. I admired his enviable nonchalance. The Camino was for him a simple escape from the stresses of the real world. Later on, I met a weathered, graying Spaniard who gave out directions in a gruff, rustic accent that matched the sleepy, sun-dried landscape of the northern Spanish plains. And there were two Danish teenagers, Peter and Markus, who were out for a summer adventure (it also happens that we're still Facebook friends).

With so many people coming together — funneling, so to speak — you are forced to mix with other people. We met while eating meals together, relaxing in the common rooms of the *albergues*, and hiking for hours on end along the trail. And the best part is that most of the time we got past the perfunctory conversation and into something much more meaningful. I remember one particularly grueling day along the hot, dry northern plains. The hike was long, maybe 18 miles, and knowing how hot it would be, we got an early start. A group of us finished early and reached the *albergue* several hours prior to opening. I wandered around the town to scope things out, purchased a baguette and large bottle of water at a local bakery, and found a shady spot under the *albergue* wall to snack. I struck up a conversation with a man nearby, another *peregrino* resting his tired feet after a blistering hike. We got to chatting. He was a Hungarian graduate student working on his Ph.D. in history. I was impressed by his intelligence, curiosity, and mastery of English. The talk turned to politics and U.S. foreign policy. To hear his perspective was enlightening. But most of all, I was engaged by his questions. Why does America have such a convoluted election process? Why does religion play such an important role in American politics? Why are we Americans so arrogant? All great questions and we learned from each other. This is what the Camino can do.

Our group also had the pleasure of running into an affable Brazilian contingent that proved true all the rumors of their countrymen's friendliness, not to mention skill with a soccer ball. By chance alone, our schedules coincided for several weeks. Each night, after dinner, one of the Brazilians pulled out his guitar and charmed us all with a soft, mysterious Bossa Nova. Those who knew the words whispered along, and those who didn't were content to sway with the gentle rhythms. Of all the people we met along the way, the Brazilians remained our closest friends. We stayed together for a week or two enjoying the Camino together. But when our schedules ceased to align, and our respective groups finally split up, one of the Brazilians offered his beloved Brazilian soccer jersey to a member of our group. It was a generous act of goodwill and friendship, the kind so frequently offered on the Camino.

One reason for building these strong relations is that most of the Camino passes through rural areas of Spain. Many of the towns are small and would most likely be abandoned if not for the economic benefits of the Camino. These towns were comprised of little more than a church, an *albergue*, a small restaurant, and a few houses. These were some of the best of all because they forced community building. There were no internet cafes or hidden corners to which one could escape. All we had for entertainment was socializing with each other.

At some point, a group member named Allie spotted a small, cheap beach ball at a local toy store. We all pitched in our coins to cover the cost of a two-dollar toy like ten-year-olds trying to buy a baseball for a summer pickup game. The ball quickly became a de facto member of our group, hitching a ride on Allie's backpack for several hundred miles. It was our version of Wilson from *Cast Away*, giving life to an otherwise austere existence. In San Juan de Ortega, for example, a game of impromptu soccer erupted into a scene of international friendship. Markus and Peter from Denmark, Phil from Zimbabwe, David and Tomás from Spain, and us, the lumbering Americans who played with more enthusiasm than skill. It was our mini World Cup boasting a field of a half-dozen nations.

As I reflect on the Camino, one question continues to linger. Can this centuries-old pilgrimage maintain the sense of community that I experienced so memorably in the summer of 2006? By all accounts, the Camino is rapidly changing, and many factors are conspiring against my hopes. The number of hikers each year continues to climb steadily. Infrastructure is constantly developing as bars, restaurants, shops, and hostels take advantage of the growing economic opportunities available. I'm sure that with these changes will come more internet cafés, more connectivity, and more technological convenience. But I hope that the Camino can maintain its character in the coming decades. The Camino is all about the dynamic community, but to do so, it must maintain a certain degree of insularity from the modern world. If hikers can maintain too much contact with their worlds outside of the Camino, they won't have the opportunity to develop the community within. And that is where all the joy emanates from.

One place I see this happening is with large groups and companies that work to support hikers along the way. We ran into at least one group of about 20 or 30 high school students. But they were too large a group to blend in and too young to venture out unsupervised. Their presence was overwhelming to the other hikers, and I was glad to move past them. In addition, a growing number of professional couriers are capitalizing on increased demand. They guide hikers along the way, make hotel or hostel reservations for their clients, and carry bags in vans. This was also troubling for me because that takes away one of the most critical aspects of the Camino: that everything you have, you carry. It's part of the experience, the adventure, the independence, the unknown. And the satisfaction is just not the same when you don't carry your belongings on your back.

So did we create an inclusive community along the way? My answer is a resounding "Yes." I met too many good people, had too many thought-provoking conversations, and made too many good friends that it is impossible to say otherwise. In a world that is shrinking in so many ways and becoming more and more a Facebook world in which all our friends, "friends," co-workers, neighbors, and relatives exist in our virtual community, we really forego the necessary conversations that are required to learn about our (real) world.

Like the modern world in which we live, everything on the Camino is dynamic. Thirty-two different *albergues* in thirty-three days. New sites and sounds. New challenges each day. New people to meet. The ebb and flow of community is never still. Now, in the fast-paced, dynamic, technology-driven "now-ness" of the 21st century, the Camino stands out, encompassing the fast-paced, dynamic world of the 21st century — but without all the technology. My hope is that the Camino can find a way to protect itself from the rapid developments of the modern world, continue to foster face-to-face human relationships, and always stay a fashionable mile or two behind.

THE REVELATIONS OF LA ISLA

Ryan Jackson

A ny story one tells about the Camino starts in the middle by necessity, as the beginning and ending of it is unclear. Yes, there were days before we started following yellow arrows, and there were days after we stopped doing so, but those do not represent the starting and stopping points of the trip. It is impossible to put our fingers on the time that we felt pushed or called or compelled or some other expression that caused us to decide to walk the Camino de Santiago. And it is possibly harder to determine the point at which we no longer feel the desire to get to the cathedral of Santiago, or even the point where we stop waking up feeling the pull of the road and the need to begin the day's walk. That is, if one ever loses that. And so, like all good writers of epic should (even those that are only epic on a personal level), I begin *in medias res*.

I was in a town called La Isla on the Camino del Norte with my walking companions Jake, Danny, and our leader/ professor George. We had walked 35 kilometers the day before on the side of a highway, and we were feeling the effects. Jake and Danny, in particular, were both having pain in their knees. In this little town which was composed of an *albergue*, a church, and fields of cows, George told Jake he had to get rid of some of the weight in his pack or he would not be able to walk all the way to Santiago. The thing that would be easiest to get along without and also remove the most weight happened to be the Bible that Jake had received as a gift from his mother before he left — an object of great emotional significance. And so, with great outflow of emotions, Jake let George take his Bible so that it could be left at the *albergue* a hundred meters or so away. I surreptitiously put the book that I had been reading in my pocket and offered to walk with George. And, as one might now anticipate, I left my book at the *albergue*, and Jake's Bible continued its journey to Santiago in my backpack.

To be honest, I hate telling that story. To recount it makes me feel like all those pilgrims who walked the Camino and immediately felt compelled to write a memoir of their magical, life-changing experience. It makes me feel self-absorbed, prideful, and silly. However, I share it now to show the power of the Camino de Santiago, and there is no better story that I have to demonstrate this than this one. It would be easy to bloat it with metaphoric and poetic language. In fact, as an English major, I would find it hard not to not do so — except that the story is about me. In a very literal sense, I was taking on the burden of my friend, which is prime for grandiose language. Add in that the burden that I happened to be helping him with was religious in nature, and the danger of pomposity increases tenfold. Indeed, it is not so hard to imagine telling that story and either subtly or outright comparing myself to Jesus carrying the cross, at least literarily. I sit writhing in discomfort writing that. My point is, though, that it is easy to do. It is an easy thing to take one's experiences on the Camino de Santiago, dress them up in language that is not unreasonable, and end up with something completely different from what was intended.

Any story told about the Camino de Santiago, unless it is about how one drank and desecrated one's way across Spain (and even then), is going to contain an element of epic-ness. It is such an otherworldly thing to do. We have airplanes if you need to travel hundreds of miles, cars if you need to go tens, and even now motorized scooters if you only need to go a few miles. To eliminate all of that, and to say that you are going to *walk* hundreds of miles? Immediately, you have changed a simple story into something epic or heroic. Worse, it is hard for you to not get caught up in it. One has accomplished something extraordinary in arriving at Santiago, and that is true. It is an experience which can and does alter you, perhaps significantly and perhaps permanently. That is certainly true. And there is a desire to explain to others and yourself what happened, how this came about, how you did this thing which others (and even yourself) expressed doubts and worries about doing. It is very easy to get wrapped up in it.

And this brings me back to my story. This is, by the way, the fourth time that I have made an attempt to write it. All previous attempts were tossed out for being too ridiculous or too conceited. It is a story that is hard to explain to people who have not had the benefit of walking the Camino. One has to take into account the fatigue that walking that much every day brings. Once when we eventually decided that we needed to end our day early to prevent debilitating injury, I slept for 14 hours. I fell asleep for a "nap" at 4 in the afternoon, I woke up at 6 the next morning. With the fatigue also comes crankiness. Everyone gets angry with everyone else at some point along the way, and if they are smart they spend that hour or two walking at a distance from people. Before I went on the Camino, I had this image of pilgrims always smiling and jovially talking with their companions and others they met along the way. They would share meals at night and settle into a peaceful sleep to wake up bright and early and full of energy. More often, one discovers a pilgrim who is exhausted, hungry, slightly irritable, and despondent at the thought of another night where his bunkmate snores so loudly that he can make the roof rattle until this same bunkmate wakes up at five in the morning to pack his bags with as much noise as possible. That is a more realistic image of the Camino, and one that I think is only fully grasped by fellow pilgrims. Further, I think only they understand that while all pilgrims feel like that at times, nearly all pilgrims are also there with kind words and encouragement for those despairing; with support and assistance for those who are hurt; with compassion and generosity for those in need. And while from the outside looking in, those actions are inexpressible in their goodness and make the viewer or reader experience awe and wonder at them. For pilgrims, though, they are the daily experience of the Camino and what it means to be part of the brotherhood of pilgrims. They are ordinary actions for us both to do and to receive. It is only extraordinary if you have not been a pilgrim. This is not to say that we expect such treatment or that we do not experience great abiding gratitude when another pilgrim helps us, but rather that it is not alien to us. For the pilgrim-as-pilgrim, it is not something to be exalted; it is something that we do by our nature.

The problem arises in that we are not always "pilgrim-as-pilgrim." Either we lapse back into our old mindset while on the Camino, or eventually it washes off of us due to our time away from that environment. In any case, it is easy to think back on our experiences with the mindset of the non-pilgrim and be simply in awe of something otherworldly — of something epic — of something heroic. And as these are thoughts about our own experiences, they quickly turn into *I* did something epic; *I* am heroic. It is a powerfully corrupting thought, and can threaten to undo all that was done on the pilgrimage as we rapidly wrap our simple stories up in metaphors. *I* am a hero. *I* carried my friend's burden. *I* carried my friend's faith. *I* gave up what *I* had to take up that of my fellow pilgrim. Because of *me*, he made it to Santiago. And who is to say that this is not true? Who would deny that claim? Fortunately, the answer is simple: the person who would deny that is the person who was there that day; the pilgrim who gave up his book to carry his friend's possession.

For you see, the story in all its heroic glory has to have all those metaphors that gloss over the truth and paint over it with eloquence. When we go back to the day itself, I was tired and muddy. I had blisters covering the bottoms of my feet so that it both hurt to walk and it hurt to stand still. And I am standing at this crossroads in the middle of God-knows-where in Spain, next to a pasture that smells of fresh manure. My friend is hurting and has to give up his book, a Bible, to which he is attached. I know how the Camino works at this point, and if I do something I regret, I will spend the next 5 hours beating myself up over it. I do not care very much about my book. Yes, I want to read it, but mostly, I've fallen asleep trying. I should take Jake's Bible instead. It was more important to him, and more to the point, I am able to. Like I said, I do not care about my book; he cares about his; I am hurting, but doing all right; he is hurting, but hitting a breaking point. That last point is probably the most important point in both my thoughts that day and in that unofficial code of pilgrim behavior: we help those who walk around us in the knowledge that one day, we *will* need help, and there will be some pilgrim there to help us.

I reflect on this now over the course of several hours to try to identify and justify my actions, but the fact is that this decision occurred in the course of several seconds. It was not a decision that had to be wrestled with. I suppose it was consciously chosen, but only in the strictest sense. I am a pilgrim — what else was I to do? It was not epic or heroic. Nor was I doing it to carry his faith or a metaphysical burden of his in any way, shape or form (regardless of whether he would say that I did so or not). The Camino does change us. While others will say that it changes us in a plethora of ways, they will all agree that it makes us, at least for a time, pilgrims. Pilgrims do things that normal people would not do. They do heroic things, epic things, and truly good things. Mostly, they do these things without the desire for a reward and without a conscious effort to ostentatiously display some aura of "goodness" about them. But for themselves, and for their own kind, these things are ordinary in the truest sense: they are intrinsic to their nature and are not especially laudable or astonishing. And while a part of me recognizes that what happened out there at La Isla was good and, in a sense, heroic, the majority of me shrugs and feels "that is what pilgrims do."

Recently, I was in a class where I shared some of my stories and feelings about the Camino. After I finished, I was asked, "Does the Camino bear any importance for your day-to-day life?" I do not know how other people in my situation would have responded to this. I do not know if I am unique or if it is something universal. But, speaking for myself, I am still a pilgrim on my way to St. James, and I hope that will never stop being the case.

HIKING THE CAMINO TRAIL

Philip Jackson

On top of a mountain, I was standing in a dense cloud, so thick that I could barely see just a few feet in front of me. Despite not having seen a trail marker for at least a mile, my grandfather and I pushed on through the rugged trail for what seemed like an eternity. Struggling, we managed to get to the bottom of the mountain, praying that we would find the trail. To our dismay, we came to realize not only that we were off the trail, but it was nowhere in sight. However, I am not the type of person to quit something once I am motivated to complete it. We pushed on, and eventually found ourselves going in the correct direction, toward Burgos, although we were not scheduled to reach the city for another day. We realized that the only way to get to Burgos was to walk on a highway against oncoming traffic on a tiny curb barely wide enough for us to walk on. We saw a construction worker on the road, and we walked over to him to ask for directions. He said something to us in Spanish which neither of us could understand, and after about 10 minutes of waving and trying to communicate, the man finally motioned for us to get into his truck. We gave him copious thanks and tried to pay him, but he refused. So there we were, riding in a truck to Burgos, thanking our lucky stars that this generous man was there to help us. This experience is something unique to the Camino. On any trail you can get hopelessly lost, but only on the Camino can you find an entire nation of generous, kind-hearted people who will go out of their way to help out someone in need.

When I walked the Camino in 2008, I was 15 years old. It was my first hike longer than an afternoon. I had no idea what to expect; needless to say, I was very excited. That summer was the beginning of a tradition for my grandpa and me, in that we now go on hiking trips each summer, and we go day hiking any chance we get. This tradition is the beginning of a never-ending journey, all started by the Camino de Santiago. Starting off in Roncesvalles, I was a 15-year-old boy, hiking just for something to do in the summer. Nearing the end of the Camino, I was maturing into a man, and I had gained a more adult outlook on life and on the world. The Camino was a true coming-of-age experience for me, and it is one I will never forget.

Walking the Camino with my grandpa was an eye-opening experience for me. Although I was 60 years younger than my grandpa, he kept up like a champion, and sometimes I thought I was the one slowing us down. Being with someone constantly for extended periods can be trying on the nerves; however it also strengthens bonds and pulls people closer. I learned more about my grandpa during our hike together than I had during the rest of my life. We remain hiking partners to this day, and we will be as long as we are both fit to hike. My grandpa and I shared experiences that we will both remember for the rest of our lives.

During my time in Spain, I grew very accustomed to running everywhere I went. I am normally not a person who runs anywhere at all, but after a couple of weeks on the trail I felt the need to run constantly. Not only was running a way to pass my extra time, but I came to enjoy the simple pleasure of it. I amazed myself with how much faster I could run than before I started the Camino, and how much longer I could run. Running became my way to clear my mind and relax at the end of my day. I remember after enjoying a coke and some tapas in a bar, I got up and was so ready to sprint out the door back to the *albergue*, I forgot to pay the owner for my snack. I was already halfway back before I realized what I had done, and I looked back to see a confused bar owner staring out the door at me. I ran back to the man, paid him, apologized, and then promptly ran back to the *albergue*.

While hiking the Camino, we saw many family groups. We met one entire family who was hiking together: a mother and father, and their two daughters. They had come all the way from Korea to do the Camino. They spoke good English, but did not speak much Spanish. I remember seeing their youngest daughter, who was maybe eight or nine years old, talking to a Spanish girl about her age. They spoke to each other in English, which they both spoke fairly well. This is the sort of thing you see on the Camino — people coming together and doing something together, regardless of cultural differences.

The *albergues* are melting pots for all different types of people, and they are a huge part of the overall experience of hiking the Camino. Sleeping in the *albergues* was a unique experience. I remember one time I woke up with my grandpa pinching my nose shut, telling me to be quiet. Apparently I had been talking in the middle of the night, as I often do. In *albergues* some of the people have rather odd sleeping habits. Some people snore in unique ways, and others like me talk or cry out in their sleep. I remember meeting one man who seemed perfectly normal until he fell asleep, at which point he would throughout the night yell nonsense. Another interesting thing about *albergues* is that almost all of them have bunk beds, usually fairly close together. I always slept on the bottom bunk, but the one time I slept on top I remember my feet would hang over the edge, and people would dodge them as they walked by.

The Camino truly does have something for everyone; no matter if you're a tourism junkie, a lover of the outdoors, or even a computer fanatic like me. The best part about it is that everyone who hikes the trail has a unique experience, even on the second or third time. My grandfather has now hiked the trail four times, and has collected three *Compostelas*. One of the unique parts about the Camino is the way it sucks you back in. I was told by one of my grandpa's old friends, with total confidence, that I would be back to do the trail again. I had my doubts at the time, but the man was right. For me, the Camino was not just a six-week trip to Spain, nor was it just a long hiking trail. The Camino is the trail that gave me my love of hiking. It is the trail that converted me into a believer in the majesty of nature. The trail gave me a desire to see what the world has to offer. In this way the Camino has more to offer than just a collection of sights and sounds. It offered me an insight into my soul, and I liked what I found.

Everyone experiences this magnificent trail differently, but at the same time we all experience it the same way. We are all moved by the amazing sights and sounds, and even more by the incredible people that we meet along the way. There are a few things in life that can change your whole outlook on the world. These things can be anything from having your first child, to something as simple as a sudden realization. When I hiked the Camino de Santiago, I gained many new memories, many new stories to tell, and most of all I gained a brand new perspective with which I look upon the world. The Camino changed me in many ways. It transformed my physical appearance as well as my mentality. Now, when I see a path going into the woods, I don't think about the lack of electricity or the lack of toilets that would have made the path undesirable to me in the past. Now, I think about where it might go, and what I might see along the way. In this way the Camino did more for me than trim down my excess weight; it also strengthened my mind, which has allowed me to see the world in a more positive light.

I believe that everyone with the ability should make a pilgrimage to Santiago de Compostela. I also believe that if I had the ability to describe exactly what the trail has done for me, anyone reading this would want to hike the Camino. This is more than just a trail; it is a spiritual pathway to enlightenment. Walking this trail was the most liberating experience I have ever been through, and I would recommend it to anyone of any age.

ABIERTA

Mallory Trowbridge

My body exhausted, I lay wearily on the top bunk of the bed as my eyes wandered over the blank four walls of the *albergue*. Rolling over, I tried to place my small pillow over my head to muffle the symphony of snoring and buffer the stench of wet feet. My eyelids were heavy but sleep did not come easily. Although I knew that the first bustling of the four o'clock crowd would come early, my head was too full to rest as the events of that evening replayed over and over in my mind.

Sitting around the common space with my classmates, we were all enjoying the company of one another. As a college group, the 10 of us had lived on the same campus for several years, but yet knew nothing of one another. The diverse nature of the group could not have been better picked by a reality TV show director. Among us we had those who represented nearly every grade school faction imaginable from jock to prep; they all were there. While the differences were extreme, the nature of our situation had brought us together and, over the first few days, we had gradually begun to gain a basic understanding of one another as we sat at night and talked among ourselves.

On this particular evening we had been talking quietly for quite a while when the first group decided it was time to retire for the evening and tip-toed their way into the room of beds. The rest of the group followed shortly after and I found myself picking up their snack wrappers before I too was to head off to bed. As I started to walk that way, I saw the hospitalera out of the corner of my eye. She coaxed me in her direction and with her tender fingers on my arm, she guided me into another room off the kitchen. She pulled out a chair and sat quietly and I followed suit. In a low voice she began to speak. I focused intently on her lips as I tried to bring meaning to her words. While I had taken notes for many years in my Spanish classes, nothing had quite prepared me for an occasion like this as I yearned to understand her.

"I know you are very special," she told me in her soft Spanish. She spoke of my beauty and strength and the perplexed nature of my stare grew. It was at that moment she asked me the question that would roll over and over in my mind for the days to come. Looking into my eyes she asked, "Do you know why you are here?"

I sat silently for a moment to ponder her question. On the surface the response seemed simple. Yes, I am here because my crazy professors thought that it would be fun to take a group of college students on a jaunt across Spain. They for some reason felt that we would enjoy the blisters and pouring rain, but as I felt her hand on mine I knew that this answer was not what she was seeking. Before I had the chance to respond she spoke again.

She told me that she knew that I was with a group, but she felt in her heart that I was different. In my eyes she could see a desire to be more, learn more and do more. She said I was here for a reason and for what it was, she could not tell me. Brushing my hair from my eyes, she told me to treasure each moment I had here. "Live each second to the fullest. When you want to scream, yell loud enough that it will echo on the other side of the ridge. When you want to cry, let the tears flow like the river. When you want to laugh, let a rich laugh bellow from deep inside. Wear your heart on your sleeve and stay 'abierta' [open] to all the Camino has to give," and with this she stood up, and I too slid my chair back from the table. She held me close and wished me well. She reminded me that I had an important purpose on this journey, and not to let it pass me by.

As my bed vibrated with each rumbling snore, I stared into the darkness as my thoughts ricocheted through my mind. Nuts, she was just a crazy old lady, pay her no notion and get some sleep; but, perhaps, there was something in what she was saying. Perhaps this journey was more than squeaking shoes, wet clothes, and a sore back. Maybe there was a reason

I was brought to this place far from home, and perhaps I had a purpose here.

When the morning crowd began to stir, I sat up slowly in my bed and rubbed my foggy eyes. I reached for my large green hiking backpack at the foot of the bed and dragged it toward me. Using the tiny flashlight from under my pillow, I rummaged through it to find the plastic storage bags within it. Pulling out a large ziplock bag, I placed my small pillow within it and squeezed out the air pushing it to the bottom of the pack in hopes that it would be dry when I reached my next destination. I then pulled the blue sack of valuables from the bottom of my purple fleece sleeping bag and set it aside. Carefully I rolled my sleeping bag tightly and wrapped it a large black hefty bag, placing it gently on top of my pillow. Finally I secured my bag of valuables and slithered down the side of the bunk bed.

My feet hit the ground and I saw that Megan was waiting with her pack ready to go. While we had only known each other for a short time, we were quickly becoming great friends, as she was one of the few among us who enjoyed the early morning life on the Camino. We headed for the light in the doorway and opened it just enough to squeeze out.

We walked along the dirt road in silence, for we had both agreed that little conversation was necessary prior to our first *café con leche*. Listening to the patter of my feet, my mind continued to wander. Climbing the first hill of the day, I marveled at the number of people ahead of us, and shot a quick glance over my shoulder to those behind us. Why were all of us here?

My thought was broken by the first *¡Buen Camino!* of the day, as we passed a couple with waves and smiles. In that moment I began to think that perhaps my own purpose here could be realized by knowing those around me. Comforted by the warmth of my morning coffee and my stomach satisfied with the sweetness of my *magdalena*, I was off with a purpose.

The first lady I came to was walking alone. "*¡Buen Camino!*" I said as I greeted her enthusiastically. She smiled and returned the greeting. I slowed my pace slightly and initiated conversation. I told her about my group and the class that had brought me here, and she quickly began to tell me about herself. As a third time *camino* walker, she could not get enough. She told me of the trials and tribulations of her own life and her recent divorce which had brought her back to the fields of Spain once more. Seeking time away from the stress of her daily life, she sought refuge in the peace of the trail and the kindness of those around her. Despite her current battles at home, she was in impressively high spirits and I found her energy contagious as we waved and parted ways nearly two hours later.

When we reached the *albergue* that night, I found that I was beginning to recognize faces of those around me. Sharing a smile and a nod we acknowledged this new-found relationship of proximity with delight. Climbing to the top bunk, I began to unpack my sack and claim my spot for the evening. As I did so, more *peregrinos* meandered in and began to do the same. I rested silently in my bed and watched intently as those around me also began to stake out their own space. Sizing them up like one would do sitting on an airplane waiting for a seat partner to arrive, I wondered who would be the one sleeping under me that night.

As soon as he walked in, my question was quickly answered. He made his way slowly through the door, and his smile accented the wrinkles on his face. He set his pack down beside my bed and gave me a wink. I returned the gesture and greeted him. While we had knowingly crossed paths many times over the last four days, we had not yet exchanged words and I soon knew why. The gentleman was from France and spoke broken English and a limited amount of Spanish. In our short conversation filled with choppy Spanglish sentences, I came to learn that he was 76 years old and had a dream of completing the entire Camino. While he had walked previously and reached Santiago from a closer starting point, he had strong ambitions to walk each section of the road beginning in France. The two years prior, he had started in France and walked for a little more than a week and then gone home. Last year he had picked up where he had left off and done just a bit more. This year he was walking for a little less than two weeks and seeing how far he could go. Eventually he said he would fill in the pieces again, but he seemed very content doing small sections of the trail and enjoying the fine company along the way.

As the lights went out, I wished the gentleman a good night and embraced the orchestra of sleeping sounds with a smile as I faded off to sleep. Morning came early and we were off again for another day. The packing routine that had seemed so foreign at first had now become routine and my friend and I were off once more. Meandering down the path, I took great joy in watching the sunrise and listening to the sounds of the forest as it began to spring to life.

The days passed quickly and I took great joy in watching the numbers on the mileage markers decrease as I came closer and closer to my destination. Finding the bright yellow arrows along the way was like being on an endless Easter egg hunt, and the thrill never seemed to wear off. Each day my eyes opened groggily to welcome the new day, and I became increasingly excited about what was before me. The sights and sounds of nature that surrounded me and the fascinating stories of those beside me made each day a new adventure as the cold and wet conditions disappeared from my mind.

The nights were often filled with time around the fire with my new-found companions, as I continued to learn more about what had brought each and every person to this place and the purpose that they felt they were to fulfill on their Camino journey and in life beyond. I met some from as far as Canada and Australia and others who had just caught a short flight from Germany and France to embark on their adventure. Some came with a spouse or companion; however, quite a few people traveled alone. While some found the Camino a place that harbored many of their religious sentiments, many simply seemed to have come to find the peace and simplicity that Camino life offered. Their professions ranged from doctors and lawyers to teachers and business owners. Some found themselves at a unique crossroads of life and seemed to be using their time as a reflective period. I enjoyed seeing pictures of their families and children that were often worn in a keychain on their pack or placed in a location within easy access. While they were all very different, each had a fascinating story to tell, and I could not get enough!

Before I knew it, thirteen days had flown by, and we were waking up on what would be our last day of hiking. I packed my things slowly that morning as sadness began to creep over me. I peered out the window in hopes that our last day would bring sun, but as the rain poured down, all dreams of clean clothes and dry feet fled my mind. We would end the walk, fittingly, just as it had been throughout our journey — wet and cold. Each step I took that day gave me a bittersweet feeling. My excitement to finally reach our destination was mounting, but the sorrow that our journey was about to end was ever present in my mind. As the rain poured down, our group trudged along with every step brining us closer to Santiago.

Sopping wet and shivering in the cold, I became increasingly eager to be done. Reaching the cathedral, the numbness of my body overtook any joy I could have felt and I yearned for a warm shower and a place to rest my weary body. After forcing a smile for a few pictures we made our way a few more blocks to the hotel where we would spend the night before attending the Pilgrim's Mass in the morning.

After a long bath and a good night's sleep, I woke up with an overwhelming sense of joy. For the first time in two weeks, I happily put on clean dry clothes and walked with my group to the Cathedral for Mass. While I had been inside many churches and attended a multitude of services in my life, this one would forever stand out in my mind.

As I gazed around me, I could not help but marvel at the magnitude of the cathedral and the throngs of people within it. As we sat in silence, my eyes wandered from face to face, and a smile crept across my face. Here I sat an ocean away from home surrounded by friends. We winked and waved quietly across the church. I listened intently as the priest read off the list of arriving pilgrims that were among us, telling us each person's nationality and starting point. I soon felt as though I could have read the list for him and even included names. These were my comrades — the ones who had helped me make it through the last few weeks. As the Pilgrim's Mass came to a close, I could not help but feel that the true Camino spirit was not above us but within us.

Later that evening, I rendezvoused with those whom I had met on the trail. We swapped stories of our last day and the loneliness of the hotel the night before. We wandered the town together and took pictures of each other as we smiled happily in front of the cathedral. We shopped in the stores and helped each other pick out gifts for loved ones back at home. As the sun began to set, we could not bear to let the evening end, and we found ourselves in a local pub for dinner. We ate and drank late into the night, savoring our last moments together. When it came time for us to finally call an end to the fun, we did so with tears in our eyes as we exchanged email addresses and promises to stay in touch and share pictures of our time together.

Returning home proved to be far more difficult than I had ever expected, for no one could truly understand the physical and spiritual journey that was the Camino. While explanation of the trip to those at home was fruitless, I found comfort in daily communication with my Camino friends. While our talks to this day have decreased, I still enjoy the Christmas cards and emails that I receive from all around the world. I continue to cherish the many memories that I created over my time as a *peregrina*, and not a day goes by where I am not thankful for the *hospitalera* who encouraged me to make the most of my journey. While our interaction was brief, her words have continued to follow me as I feel they not only embody the spirit of the Camino but also express an approach to everyday life that brings an unsurpassable happiness to all those who live *abierta*.

¡POR ARRIBA!

Megan K. Drohan

The first meeting: mainly informative, so you know what you could be getting yourself into. But I didn't have much of a choice. You have to understand that when I came to college, I did the unthinkable, I decided to actually apply myself — which seems very foreign to a lot of college students nowadays. So I chose three majors (yes, three): French, Spanish, and International Relations. Now, I'll be lucky to escape with my sanity after five years considering the hectic and overloaded schedule I set myself up for by choosing this path. And thus, I knew that I *had* to do this trip, no matter what it was. I didn't have time to spend a semester in a Spanish-speaking country and I didn't have time to wait around for another required May-term course. So I listened intently as my professors described a month-long trip to Spain, hoping that it would be something I would love.

Week one: Madrid, stay in a hotel, see museums, keep a journal. *Perfect! I love history, I'm familiar with city life, and who could complain about the easy access to night clubs?* Week two: Salamanca, stay with a host family, attend classes, tour the city, and get used to Spanish life. *Even better! This will improve my Spanish so much, and I'm sure the classes will be a breeze.* Weeks three and four: hike the Camino de Santiago, stay in *albergues*, sweat like a pig, use public showers, walk through mud and God-knows-what-else, and visit a big church at the end. *WHAT?! No, no, no and more NO. I'm not made for this! I signed up for an academic trip, not an outdoor adventure!*

Everyone else seemed really excited to do this — all of it. Weeks one and two would be amazing, that I knew. But what I also knew was that I am not an outdoorsy person. Sure, I like looking at nature in pictures, and I might even go out in it for an hour, maybe two, but I am not the kind of person who drops out of the real world to go on a hike. I drop out of the real world for shopping, or a nap, or a good Facebook session, not to absolve myself of sin by becoming one with the earth! Just the thought of it makes me cringe! But everyone else in the room is asking, "What do I need to bring?" and "Should I get hiking boots?" and "What if it rains?" while I am just shaking my head in disbelief. I won't, I mean, I can't, there's just no way. But in my heart of hearts, I knew that I had to go; a Spanish major requires a trip abroad, and this was the only time I had to do it. I had no other choice but to go. Nonetheless, I could not ease my mind's concerns about all the reasons I shouldn't be going on this trip. No exaggeration here: I am honestly the most ill-prepared, least-experienced, and unwilling candidate on earth to hike the Camino de Santiago.

This isn't just some little walking trip either, mind you. We will be starting in León. That means I will be walking every step of that 180-mile distance between there and Santiago. Not to mention that it's the rainy season in Spain during the month of May, there are mountains to climb and descend, there is mud and animal excrement everywhere, bugs attack from every direction, oh and by the way, you are carrying a good 20-30 pounds on your back throughout all of this. I don't know whose idea of a cruel joke this was, but I was not enthused about it. In fact, I was *dreading* it, and here is why…

I was raised in the suburbs of Chicago, in one of its most esteemed and well-off suburbs, as a matter of fact. What was important in Wheaton, Illinois, when I was growing up consisted of the three A's: Abercrombie, Athletics, and Academics. As a product of that environment, I did everything I could to satisfy the three A's. There was nothing wrong with the three A's. Sure, they are somewhat materialistic and elitist — but honestly, what suburb isn't? Obviously, my hometown left much to be desired in terms of character building. For instance, about the closest I ever got to camping was Girl Scout camp in fourth grade, which lasted a whole five days, by the way, and I hated every second of it. And worst of all, you aren't just a product of this environment anymore, you *become* it; you live it, you breathe it, and you feed it every day, so that you think that there is nothing bigger out there — that this suburban, protected, materialistic life is what it's all about — what anyone could ever dream of. So let's face it, my environment didn't exactly prepare me for things like hiking or fishing or worst of all, camping. I made my best effort at wearing what was popular in high school — North Face jackets, jeans with pre-made holes, shirts with some name brand stretched across the front like a billboard, all of that great stuff. And I played sports, a lot of sports — there was no way you could become popular at my high school if you didn't play a sport. Although I was a fair athlete, I wasn't amazing at anything in particular so I jumped around a lot — ice skating, ballet, softball, soccer, volleyball, and track. But the point was that I at least played. And then of course, there is the ever important aspect of academics. Not being a genius, I learned early on that school was more about working hard than being smart, so that's what I did all the way through high school, and now, in college. So, essentially the three A's were the focus of my life until I left Wheaton for college in 2006.

So clearly reason number one for me to avoid this trip is that I am the least prepared person to trek across a country. But secondly, I am not religious. And by "not religious" I mean that is what my mom told me to tell people so that they wouldn't judge me. Truthfully, I am somewhere between agnostic and atheist. I made a decision a long time ago that religion just wasn't for me, and I've never looked back since. But now I'm about to go on a *religious* pilgrimage. For those of you who don't know what that means, this pilgrimage was an extremely long hike to a Catholic cathedral. In the pre-modern era, pilgrimages often served as temporal punishment for crimes or acts unbefitting a Christian. Nowadays, people often walk the Camino to become closer to God by showing their commitment to religion. Obviously, not too many atheists decide to pack their bags and start walking across Spain to show their loyalty to a God which they don't believe in. Nonetheless, there I was, preparing myself to do just that — not exactly something on my list of things to do before I die. And there you have reason number two.

I mentioned earlier all the sports that I played before college, right? Well let's just say that all those years of being athletic took quite a toll on my body. I have a lot of recurring injuries, particularly ankle problems, that tend to resurface every year or so in the form of a bone fracture. A lot of my friends like to call me "fragile." In fact, I showed up to the second meeting about our May-term class with a broken ankle, crutches and all. My doctor actually told me to cancel my trip because my ankle wouldn't be healed yet, but as I said, I had no real choice but to go, unless I wanted to drop my Spanish major. Seeing as I wasn't about to drop something I had worked so hard for, I decided to suck it up and go. But I knew that a two-week long hike would be painful and miserable for me, which wasn't exactly the best motivation. And that's reason number three.

Now there are a million other minor reasons not to do this that were running through my head: I had a very limited financial situation, I had no one that I was close with going on the trip, I hate public restrooms, and many other things. But the main three were my "girliness," my lack of religion, and the probability of reinjuring myself. Needless to say, this was not my dream getaway. At the time, it seemed like more of a nightmare than anything else. But before I knew it, I had gotten my cast taken off, had packed my bags, and was boarding an international flight at Dulles Airport, destination: Madrid.

Throughout the time we spent in Madrid and Salamanca, I just kept hoping that something would interrupt our plans for the Camino. Every time I glanced around at my stuff, the only thing that I really took note of was my bright-green hiking backpack. It served as a constant reminder of the total and complete humiliation that was to come. I didn't even want to look at it, much less put it on. All I could think about was how much fun I was having in Madrid and Salamanca and that the Camino would spoil it for me. I just kept thinking: *I'm not ready for this, I'm* **so** *not ready for this.* But finally the day came that we had to leave Salamanca for León. Our class checked into the very first *albergue* of the trip, and I knew that it was inevitable now. I was going to hike the Camino de Santiago.

The first day wasn't nearly as bad as I thought it would be. It was hot and 25 kilometers never seemed so long, that was for sure, but it really wasn't terrible. During the first two weeks of our time in Spain, I had gotten really close with a girl named Mallory. Talking to her somehow made the walk so much better and I was grateful for her friendship. Day two was a completely different story. It was rainy and cold and muddy. It was the epitome of why I did not want to go on this trip. Within the first fifteen minutes I was soaked through and covered up to my knees in muck. But then, just to top it all off, I managed to fall on a pile of rocks halfway through the day's hike. All I kept thinking about was that this day had really exemplified my reasons for not coming: 1. *If I was supposed to be covered in mud, then I would have been born a pig;* 2. *My knee is swollen, bleeding, and really painful; and* 3. *If there was some sort of God out there, He would not put me through this. Great, just great.*

It wasn't until day five that my opinions about the Camino really began to change. Day five was our first day in the mountains. The hiking was extremely difficult, but the views were breathtaking. I had never seen nature like this: pure, unadulterated nature. It was absolutely magnificent. It was then that all of my reasons not to do this walk went out the window. I didn't care how muddy or sweaty or pained or non-religious I was, this was worth it. But day six made sure to test that strength by introducing me to a nasty case of tendonitis in my ankle. Mallory, a serious runner, suggested that I take a cab to the next town so that I wouldn't injure myself further. By this point, some of the other people in our group had been taking cabs from town to town because of their injuries and I can't lie, it was a pretty tempting offer. But I knew that taking a cab would mean that I would miss out on everything that I would have seen otherwise. So I re-taped my ankle, stopped for a coffee break, and kept going. I know that health-wise this wasn't the best decision to make, but I couldn't help myself. I didn't want to miss out on the Camino. I never thought that I would hear those words escape my mouth, but they did, and it was true. This was the most physically and emotionally demanding thing I had ever done, but I also realized that this would be the experience of a lifetime.

The absolute pinnacle point of this trip was day eleven and day twelve. We had been hiking up hills and mountains for days, but we were never really looking down at much. It was during these two days that we were literally on top of the mountains — it seemed like you could see forever in every direction. I had honestly never felt so empowered in my entire life as I did when I was looking down on the valleys of Galicia. Mallory and I kept looking at each other and asking, "Is this real?" And it was, it really was! Then we would shout, "¡Por arriba!" In Spanish this translates to something like "Go higher!" but for us, it also signified pushing ourselves harder so that we could see even more.

When we reached the *albergue* that afternoon, we met up with some of our fellow students who had taken cabs — because of injuries for some, laziness for others. Mallory and I sat down and ordered a *ron y coca* (rum and Coke) to ease the pain in our muscles while the others asked how the day was. We tried to explain just how amazing it was, but we couldn't seem to put it into words, so we showed them all our pictures. It was then that one of the people in the group turned to me and said, "How can you do all of this and have seen all of God's beauty and *not* believe?" Despite the fact that this person had taken cabs practically the entire way because he was too lazy to walk and hadn't seen anything that Mallory and I had, I tried to take his question seriously. And you know, I came to the realization that for me, at least, this trip didn't need to be about religion or about God. This trip meant so much to my own personal human experience and my own spirit that I didn't need it to be for something greater. I was happy that I did it for me and nothing else. For some that is not the case; they have a need to fulfill a purpose that seems greater than themselves. But for me, in that moment, I felt that I had served a greater purpose — I had overcome all the reasons that should have kept me from going on this pilgrimage and had become a willing participant in the greatest character-building experience of my life. My greater purpose was to discover things about myself that I never had known.

After thirteen long, hard days of hiking through mountains, mud, manure, rocks, and rain, we all arrived in Santiago. In the end, only four students (out of our group of ten students) walked the entire 180 miles, and shockingly, I was one of them. This had been one of the most fulfilling and rewarding episodes of my life. Despite all of the reasons why I shouldn't have ever walked the Camino, I did. Somehow that old saying "you can't teach an old dog new tricks" didn't apply here. I overcame all the things that were holding me back, without the help of anyone else. For the first time in my life, I felt deserving. So the lesson here is that no matter what your preconceptions are, you'll never know until you try. And let's face it, if I can hike the Camino de Santiago, then I think that just about anyone can. When all of us went out the last night to celebrate, one of the guys in our group said to me, "You really surprised me. I never in a million years thought that you could have done this." That still remains one of the greatest compliments I have received in my entire life.

FINDING MYSELF IN SPAIN

Tim Price-O'Brien

Ever been in a time machine? I have. The Camino de Santiago catapults its unwitting *peregrinos* back through centuries at a time, rediscovering an era of knights and honor, of God and faith, all on a quest ultimately to seek out themselves. In May 2008, I traveled 180 miles of the Camino by foot with a student group led by my college professors. This has been one of my finest adventures; indeed each day was its own adventure, as I encountered magnificent landscapes, enlightening company, and an inner strength on which I had never called before.

As I made my way through Spain, I recorded my daily travels and discoveries in a journal. Two days in particular, halfway though the trip, I now consider a highlight of my Camino. On the first day, unusually sunny, we were marching steadfastly through the mountains, all uphill, to the small settlement known as Rabanal. The hospitality of this town to its pilgrims shall always be a fond memory of my time in Spain. We were warmly welcomed at the *albergue* El Pilar, whose owners happily mingled with pilgrims who milled about washing clothes, enjoying their dinner, or playing with the *albergue's* little dog. One of the owners even cured pilgrims' feet, blistered from weeks of rocky terrain. I waited patiently along with other students in our group for my feet to be treated, watching the *hospitalera* work quickly, unfazed by the nasty blisters of some of the less fortunate pilgrims.

At seven that evening, pilgrims were invited to a small church in town to attend a nightly service given by the three monks of Rabanal, who sang traditional Gregorian chants. As we all huddled close together inside the church, gathered around the monks, we realized our shared sense of community. I observed the other onlookers around me, and we all stood impressed by the perfect harmony and steady rhythm of the monks' well-practiced song. What to these practitioners of faith was a daily ritual, to us was an encounter with history and culture. Together we were humbled by the power of their sheer faith, all inspired by centuries-old traditions played out before our modern minds. The Camino has a special quality that motivates us to discover at once each other and ourselves.

The travels of my second memorable day brought us to the highest point on the Camino. Magnificent does not begin to describe the perception of our surroundings. We marched boldly along the path through the rolling hills covered in dry gray-green brush and dotted with faded stone buildings and blue wildflowers. We gazed with wonder at the majestic mountain ranges in the distance. So far from the busy hustle of the fast-paced modern world, we walked ever farther without thinking how or why. Indeed we transcended our physical limits when our spirit had reached the top of the world.

At the highest point of the Camino stands a pillar with an iron cross, known as the *Cruz de Ferro*, on an impressive mound of stones placed by pilgrims who pass this pinnacle. Pilgrims traditionally bring a stone from their home along and leave it here to join the many others. Our group took time here to pause and take in our accomplishment. Many hours of unwavering strength had earned us this moment of rest and personal fulfillment. It seemed that we had only begun our pilgrimage when we were already at the point to begin downhill.

Before beginning our descent, we met Tomás, "the last of the Knights Templar," an eccentric figure who has taken on the duty of offering pilgrim hospitality along one of the more difficult sections for its *peregrinos*. Tomás has a little site on the mountain with signs pointing to cities around the world. Here, this last Knight Templar meets pilgrims and offers them encouragement and occasionally suggestions for a smooth remainder of their travels. This historical excursion lifted our spirits as we started the rigorous descent through the mountains, walking until 4 p.m. when we reached Molinaseca. Although we had planned to continue our day's travels a few miles farther, we recognized our need to accept gratefully the opportunity to rest, knowing that by the time we reached the next town there might not be space at the *albergue*.

In retrospect, had we stayed on our expected course, I might not have enjoyed what I consider the most special moment of my Camino. At an hour quite early by Spanish standards, I chanced to be looking for dinner in town at the same time as four pilgrims I had met along the way, all of different nationalities: Chris, from the United States; Matthew, from Holland; Lucio, from Portugal; and Dana, from Denmark. We collectively decided on a Spanish homestyle restaurant that offered more traditional dishes. As we entered, we realized quickly that we were the only patrons — it was much too early for dinnertime. In fact, the cook, who after a while came in and greeted us, had been at home gardening pepper plants. She came in, making us feel at home, reciting to us the entire menu herself and insisting that we enjoy some extra eggs with our dinner (unlike Americans, Spaniards often have eggs with lunch or dinner, sometimes adding them to a salad, for example).

Today when I think about what the Camino means for me, I remember how our dinner group's eclectic mix of *peregrinos* on a common journey sparked unique conversation that could only have happened in this particular moment. To listen to Europeans debate the values and consequences of the European Union brought to life my formerly uninspired book-learning. In other words, I appreciated the value of a fresh perspective, for after all what to Americans remains a peripheral academic interest to the rest of the world may be major contemporary politics. As outsiders in Spain now having dinner together at a homey Spanish restaurant, we also touched on Spanish culture, sharing our responses to Spanish art. Our Dutch friend remained unimpressed, praising non-Spanish painters whose work was convincingly realistic, while the Portuguese pilgrim saw greater value in art that conveys the feelings of the artist, insisting that we should judge paintings according to faithful individual expression. The cultural distinctions evident in this debate were striking and could have only been witnessed in this extraordinary gathering of five *peregrinos* who have taken home shared perspectives of Spain and the world.

In time, I have come to reflect on and appreciate my own growth during the Camino. I realized how I stretched past my comfortable boundaries simply for the satisfaction of learning and seeing. With each seemingly tiny step, I observed the snowy but heavily forested mountains on the horizon, the distant valleys below us, the pines and the boulders and the flowers along our path, the gorgeous little mountain towns and their simple, pure people. I felt guided more than ever before, not by my legs weary from miles of rocky terrain, but by my heart. As I followed the path of so many before me and so many to come, I became every *peregrino*, yet came back to myself. And now, as I sit in my American comforts far from the rugged mountains of the Iberian Peninsula, I still feel moved by the memory of pushing my physical limits to tread many miles through the Spanish countryside. I also shall always be humbled by the rich history and gracious hospitality shown to us by the Spanish people. By whisking us away to a simpler era, compelling us to draw our physical and social surroundings in a new light, the Camino shall timelessly enrich the lives of its pilgrims as it did mine. ¡*Buen Camino*!

BROKE ON THE CAMINO PORTUGUÉS

Andrew Talbot Squires

It wasn't supposed to be that kind of trip — broke on the Camino Portugués — but my friend Cullen had lost his wallet with all his cash and his debit card a few days earlier. We had just finished our spring semester abroad, Cullen in Madrid and I in Sevilla. With little desire to return home, Cullen and I had decided to fly north to Santiago de Compostela, wind our way down the coast to Tui, walk the Camino Portugués five days back to Santiago, and then continue another five days out to Finisterre on the coast.

I had walked the Camino Francés while in high school, so I already had a pretty clear idea of what was needed. However, there was of course Cullen to consider. Since Cullen's only shoes were a pair of Vans skateboarding shoes, he asked if he could borrow my hiking boots. But then, *I* would have had no shoes to wear. We finally agreed that we would rotate days between wearing my hiking boots and wearing my sandals. The fact that my shoes were two sizes larger than Cullen's apparently wasn't a problem.

We flew to Santiago and then continued by bus on to Tui, a Spanish city on the Portuguese border. As we sat on the bus, we contemplated our money situation. I had enough money to walk the Camino and pay for the night train from Santiago to Madrid before boarding my flight home. But now Cullen had no money, so we would have to split my remaining money between the two of us. This would not be an extravagant trip.

We arrived in Tui on a beautiful afternoon about 20 minutes before the church opened, so we waited outside to get our *credenciales* and then headed to the nearly-empty *albergue* a few blocks away. We felt a bit like imposter pilgrims as *peregrinos* who had walked that day from Rubiães in Portugal trickled in, sweaty and dirty, so we headed down to the supermarket to pick up a combination lunch-dinner and walked the three-and-a-half kilometers to Valença so that we could say we started in Portugal. Sitting on the cannons of the fortress, we snacked on bread and cheese and looked north to where we would be walking the following morning. I realized this was the first time I had walked on my own and the first time to follow this route. I shared with Cullen what this walk would be like — following yellow arrow and shell markers, sharing experiences with other pilgrims, and meeting people who lived along the route.

From the beginning, I liked the Camino Portugués. I had been expecting the norm on the French route — a densely packed *albergue*, with the infamous plastic bags beginning to rustle at 5:45 a.m. as pilgrims got ready to race off to the next *albergue*. So I was surprised when I instinctively jerked awake at 6:30 a.m., and looking around the *albergue*, saw that all three of our roommates were still asleep. I drifted in and out of sleep until everyone began slowly waking up at 7:30 a.m. and lazily packing. I could get used to this, I thought. We walked the uphill route out of Tui, following the sparsely marked yellow arrows to our destination, Redondela, 30 kilometers away. We breakfasted on a large quantity of *magdalenas*, absurdly priced at a euro for about 2,000 calories of oily, sweet breakfast cake. There were few pilgrims on the road. At Tui there were only three others at the *albergue*: an ancient German couple who, I knew, we would probably never see again as we were walking 30 kilometers, and a young guy from the Czech Republic who spoke good English. We somehow never exchanged names, so after two days Cullen and I simply took to calling him Javier between ourselves, an arbitrary choice. We met him that morning at an intersection which had a road going left and a road going right. The only arrow pointed straight ahead into a field, so we bonded over consulting our guidebooks and complaining about the lack of yellow arrows.

While anyone who walks the Camino knows of the friendship among pilgrims which naturally occurs, especially after seeing the same faces day after day, this phenomenon was ever stronger on the Camino Portugués. With only four or five pilgrims staying at each *albergue*, everyone immediately became a collected family, even if it was limited to smiles and gestures with the non-English speaking Germans. The approach into Redondela included about an hour of walking through what must be one of Spain's finest industrial parks, and while interesting, the tarmac and concrete jungle in 90-degree heat became a bit tedious. Perhaps such walking encouraged our first-day legs to arrive in Redondela before the *albergue* opened at 1 p.m. Although three euros a night for the stay was a pittance, Cullen and I were still restricted to eating from grocery stores — even the ten euro *menú de peregrino* was out of our price range considering the number of days we had remaining on the Camino. In the *albergue* we met up with Javier, and surprisingly, the older German couple who arrived late in the afternoon, steadily and still with energy. After a college-student meal of pasta and vegetables, we stood on the second-floor balcony of the *albergue* looking out on the town. I realized it is easy to become enamored of Spanish society. Teens lazily rode bikes across the bridge which bisects the river, well-dressed couples strolled along the sidewalks, and small cafés were filled with regulars who spent their evenings sipping wine.

We headed out the next day on an easier 20-kilometer walk to Pontevedra, although our sore second-day legs made it feel almost as difficult as our first day. But we were rewarded with occasional glimpses of the *rías*, rivers flooded by the sea, a view never found on the Camino Francés. As we walked through the small hamlets along the Camino Portugués, we found that people were friendlier and more interested in talking to us. We followed a fairly lax schedule, usually stopping around 10 a.m. for a *café con leche*, which we felt our budget — we were in Spain after all — must allow. Usually arriving around 1 or 2 p.m., we would snack instead of eating the typical enormous Spanish lunch, and save our appetites for a large dinner, which we could make our only big meal of the day. By Pontevedra, we began to get into the Camino rhythm, our bodies adjusting to the (fairly) early mornings and long walks, and we began to see the same faces again and again. Our Czech friend continued with us, and the ancient German couple whom I knew we would never see again after Tui resolutely kept the same pace as a pair of 20-year-olds. We were definitely the youngest pilgrims on the Camino that we saw — our timing in very early June must have placed us just ahead of schools ending — and our choice of a less traditional route clearly played a role in the pilgrim population.

It is interesting how perceptions shift while on the Camino — our biggest concern as we lazed in the yard behind the *albergue* in Pontevedra was the lack of an *albergue* in Caldas de Reis, which was a logical 21 kilometers away. As we absolutely lacked the euros to afford a hotel in Caldas de Reis, our only option seemed to be to walk to the small hamlet of Briallos, which strangely had an *albergue*, but was only a 17-kilometer walk. Yet after a roundtable discussion in broken English, gestures, and Spanish with Javier and the German couple, we felt our spirits lifted because they were also headed to Briallos. The next morning turned into a particularly hot day, and we followed our usual rhythm of running into our fellow pilgrims.

We were the last ones out of the *albergue*, but after several hours we passed the German couple, who appeared to wake up quite early in order to make it to the *albergue* before the sun reached its apex. Javier would usually start a bit earlier than we did, and we would walk with him for a while, but he stopped frequently, so by the end of the day, Cullen and I were alone. This also happened to be the time we were both the hottest, most tired, and most likely to become temporarily annoyed by each other's constant company. We usually passed this worst part of the day getting into arguments over trivial and philosophical issues. That morning in Pontevedra, Cullen had left his favorite hat in the *albergue*, which sparked a debate

154

over whether one should hold sentimental value to material objects which are easily lost. This argument of course expanded *ad infinitum*, so we were both secretly glad that we ran into a group of four loud and jovial Spanish women. They were eager to talk, and explained that they were all from the Canary Islands, and unsurprisingly for Spain, had vacation time and had decided to hike the Camino. We stopped for a break with them and were happily offered *chorizo bocadillos*. They were, however, walking on to Caldas de Reis, so after getting ahead of them that day, we never saw them again. This is part of the culture of the Camino — you meet strangers, share food and conversation, and never see them again.

Cullen and I arrived at the *albergue* in Briallos a bit past one, and were dismayed to see that it didn't open until 4 p.m. We stashed our backpacks inside the gate of the *albergue*, and, as Briallos had absolutely no restaurants or shops, walked the four kilometers into Caldas de Reis. We decided to splurge on a *menú de peregrino*, which at ten euros each represented what we had been spending in two days for lodging and food.

By now, we had about 100 euros between us. This remaining money had to get us two more days to Santiago, and then four days out to Finisterre. We had to pay for the bus from Finisterre back to Santiago, and Cullen had to buy a train ticket back to Madrid, and then find lodging for another two days after that before his flight. Cullen, as a math major, astutely calculated that we didn't have enough money to make it home. We could have become like pilgrims I have seen on later trips on the Camino, who make it a point to spend no money and make their way by handouts or donations from others. We decided instead to email Cullen's dad, asking him to deposit 100 dollars into my account so we could make it back. I got the impression from Cullen that it wasn't guaranteed his father would actually deposit the money, as perhaps pleas for money were not something new in the family. There was also a time factor to consider, as we at least needed the money before we got to Finisterre. Walking back to Briallos, we realized that our restaurant meal was a foolish waste of our money, and after talking and thinking excitedly about this, we also realized that we were walking on the completely wrong road. We had already walked about a kilometer, and at a road crossing, turned off on a road that seemed to be headed in the direction we believed Briallos might be. After another several kilometers, we realized that we were really lost. We had been walking on the pavement at 4 p.m. in full sun for nearly an hour, which didn't help, and as it was siesta, there was no one to ask for directions. Cullen wanted to continue walking up a steep road, which I knew wasn't the right way. He walked on ahead as I waited, but after five minutes, like a child left behind by his friends going into a haunted house, I decided to follow anyway. I caught up with Cullen after a few minutes, just as we crested a hill which offered a beautiful view of the valley below us. Nestled at the bottom of the valley, we saw the unmistakable outline of Briallos and our *albergue*. Relieved, we laughed at how our sense of direction had led us to walk six kilometers up a mountain. We arrived in the valley at 5 p.m., our four-hour lunch and walk over, where the rest of our Camino group — Javier and the German couple — were the only other pilgrims.

Regardless of the length of a Camino trip, the last day into Santiago is always filled with anticipation. Yet after walking mostly through towns, one's slow arrival into the city of Santiago always seems so long, as the city can be seen for many kilometers before you are even close. Having stayed at the ghost town of Monte de Gozo previously, I had always walked into the Plaza de Obradoiro in the early morning, where my mother and I were among the only ones in such an enormous plaza. The Cathedral had thus always seemed stark and cold. This time, walking down the cobblestoned streets of Santiago in the hot sun of the mid-afternoon, Cullen and I finally turned the corner into a Plaza de Obradoiro filled with people, yet still dominated by the Cathedral. After the mandatory pictures in front of the Cathedral, we quickly picked up our *Compostelas* and took the long walk out to the Seminario Menor *albergue*. While perfectly acceptable, the sheer size of the Seminario Menor made it feel like a cross between a minimum-security prison and a maze. We locked our backpacks in our bedside lockers and wove our way back outside in search of a grocery store. While the excitement of the day was our arrival in Santiago, there was also the added excitement that Cullen's dad had deposited 100 dollars into my account, giving us a new lease on travel, but still no escape from our penury.

The walk out of Santiago always feels a bit strange to me, almost like running in a race and continuing to run after crossing the finish line, while everyone else basks in the completion. The enormous spires of the Cathedral can be seen for several kilometers as one walks out of Santiago and back into the mountains; what a strange experience to be walking away from what so many walk toward! We arrived at the *albergue* a little after 1 p.m. Shockingly, there was already a long line of pilgrims formed outside, and while used to such realities on the Camino Francés, we knew that there were only 30 beds available. The *hospitalera* began writing down names, filling the 30 spaces. Cullen was #28 and I was #29. There were around 15 people behind us who had to either walk on to a hotel or walk back to a hotel, as the municipality places a strict limit on the number of pilgrims, apparently for insurance purposes. The *hospitalera* did however let an extra injured man stay, and apparently I looked like a good candidate for sleeping on tile, so I was asked to give up my bed and sleep on the floor, which I acquiesced to.

We sat around and listened to the pilgrim talk. Everyone was clearly in race mode, as the *albergue* at Olveiroa had only 34 beds and was in an isolated area. Some complained that while they got a bed at Negreira, the others who had been denied a bed had walked on and would thus be ahead in the next day's race. The group of Spaniards in our room said they were getting up at 4 a.m. in order to get an hour or two ahead of everyone else. Cullen and I looked at each other, and went to ask the *hospitalera* about buses to Finisterre. The Camino we had been enjoying was one of leisurely walking and seeing other pilgrims as company and friends rather than rivals. Walking in the dark for two hours in order to secure a place to stay seemed over the top. There were no buses until the late afternoon to Finisterre, although there was an 8:30 a.m. bus to

Muxía, which the *hospitalera* said was also a small coastal town and very pretty. There was also a 30-kilometer route between Finisterre and Muxía which we could walk. Although we knew nothing more about it, we were both standing in front of "Bar Juan" at 8:15 a.m. waiting for the bus. Our late departure granted me almost four hours of sleep in a bed, after one of the Spaniards had literally picked me up off the floor while I was asleep and plopped me in his bed as they left. I hope *they* got a bed that night. We arrived in Muxía a few hours later on a beautiful sunny day and climbed the hill overlooking the town to see how picturesque it was. Climbing to the top of the hills which overlook the town also reveals what a narrow strip of land Muxía sits on, yet this fragility seemed apt for a town on the *Costa de la Muerte*. After seeing the rat race on the Camino, we didn't feel comfortable staying at the *albergue* as we hadn't walked, so we got a hotel at a pilgrim price of 15 euros each and spent the afternoon exploring the coastline around Muxía.

My train from Santiago to Madrid left the next night at 10 p.m., so we walked down to the bar which had the bus schedule posted. There was a 9:30 a.m. bus to Santiago which I planned on taking, and a 10:00 a.m. bus to Finisterre which Cullen would take and then head back to Santiago the following day. We divided our remaining money, leaving me with 15 euros — 7 euros for the bus ride back, and the remaining 8 to eat lunch and dinner before reaching the Madrid airport the following morning. We had cut our money situation close.

We awoke the next morning and walked down to the bus station all packed. Cullen and I glanced at the bus schedule again for extra measure, and suddenly realized it was Sunday. While the bus schedule for Monday through Saturday was the same, on Sunday, there was no bus to Finisterre at all, and the only bus to Santiago was at 2 p.m. Our pilgrim attitude had made the days of the week of little importance, but we paid the consequences this day. We quickly reassessed our situation. I could still make it back to Santiago in plenty of time, but Cullen had to figure out what to do. He decided to hike the 30 kilometers to Finisterre and then continue on to Santiago the next day as planned. In our last moment together, I took off my hiking shoes on the sidewalk and gave them to Cullen so he could hike.

Of course it started raining about an hour later, and I thought of Cullen hiking through the rain as I sat in a café nursing a *café con leche* for an hour. As the bus drove out of Muxía, the rain stopped and the sun returned, and I spent a somewhat lonely but introspective evening in Santiago, until my night train pulled out at 10:30 p.m. I climbed into my compartmentalized bunk bed with two other half-asleep Spaniards, and tried to sleep. The constant movement of the train, the sound of the train's whistle, and the frequent stops made sleep almost impossible. It did, however, give me a chance to reflect. When I had walked the Camino previously, a *menú de peregrino* for lunch and a *café con leche* (or several) each morning were the norm. While more money, if we seriously needed it, was only another embarrassed phone call away, it was an interesting change to live on such a strict budget. Historically, the pilgrimage was not a vacation for the wealthy but a time of atonement for all people. Chaucer's *The Canterbury Tales* reveals this diversity, so perhaps such a trip was closer to the reality for many medieval pilgrims walking in the past. Walking the Camino Portugués also distanced us from the crowds of people, and it felt much more like simply walking through Spain than actually being on a crowded route. This monetary and environmental simplicity allowed me greater opportunity to reflect on what a pilgrimage really means — a journey into one's self. There I discovered that shoes, beds, and meals matter less than opening up to the possibilities the Camino offers.

ON GETTING LOST...

Michael Burriss

Pola Dura de la Tercia is starting to look awfully small (not that it was all that big to begin with). The climb is steep, the path not really a path at all. We are continuing our trek across the Camino de San Salvador which will eventually lead us to Oviedo. However, Oviedo seems like a long way away. Sometimes when you are exhausted and tired, you just want to be there at the next destination. Thinking like that is the opposite of Camino thinking. Since this is only my fifth day of walking, I haven't quite settled back into that old Camino mentality. It has been six years since I last walked the Camino Francés in the winter. I remember that it took me about a week to get "used" to walking 20+ kilometers a day. It snowed and sleeted almost constantly once we got to Galicia. It was cold and temperatures were near freezing. However, by the time we reached Galicia we had found our pace and rhythm. The Camino had already cast its spell on us.

Now, it seems like this impossible hill is insurmountable. How do we get up it? The trails for most of the Camino de San Salvador are rough, sometimes even non-existent. Carlos, Kaitlyn, and I arrive at the top of a green hill riddled with pebbles and patchy thorn bushes. We have not seen a marker for a while now. We are thinking that we are following a path, but we get to this hill and it seems like the Camino just stops and meshes with the rest of the spectacular scenery. We are way high up and are looking down the hill (which could really be considered a small mountain) and to the left, right, and in front of us there is nothing but valleys and more "small mountains." We cannot see a sign anywhere. Naturally, one of the first emotions we experience is a twinge of fear. Are we lost? What do we do? How do we find our way out of this?

Carlos suggests that we each go in different directions. I will go down the hill, Kaitlyn, my girlfriend, will go to the left and Carlos to the right. We are so high up that I can soon see both of them down in the valley going their respective ways. I then proceed down the hill. However, because of the incline of the hill, I cannot walk down easily on my feet. I have to lean backwards, and with my trusty Camino *bordón* in hand, I make my way one foot at a time. Before I take a step, I make sure that the *bordón* is firmly in the ground in front of me. After some time, I make it down the hill and can see Kaitlyn and Carlos on each side of the hill a good way out in each direction. I continue walking and still do not see a sign! I yell at the top of my voice that I did not find anything. Kaitlyn yells the same, but Carlos is waving and yelling that we should follow the way he has taken. Has he possibly found a marker and a way out? We go over to him — he has not found a marker but rather another mountainous-looking hill that has a well-worn foot path leading up its side.

However, maybe it is just my lack of physical dexterity or maybe just inexperience, but I cannot make it up the hill without getting on my hands and knees and literally pulling myself up little by little. I normally do not frighten easily, but we are so high up and my pack weighs so much (13 kilos almost!) that I am thinking that I am going to tumble down the hill. Kaitlyn is waiting at the bottom of the mountain to see if I can make it up before she attempts her climb. Carlos has already found a flat spot halfway up where he is resting. I eventually make it up to that spot out of breath and my hands bleeding from the "sticklers," as I call them, and sit down. Kaitlyn, more frightened of heights than I am, makes it up little by little and conquers her fears. We all look at each other like, What just happened? This trail is insane. We are doing all this and it may not even be the right way. Why are we doing this?

Well, you know what? We make it up the rest of the hill only to come to somewhat of a clearing. It has undulating, green valleys that stretch as far as the eye can see. To the right the green pasture starts to turn white from the snow that is still blanketing it. The snow has not melted because of its geographical surroundings which have trapped the cold air in and blocked much of the day's heat, preserving this beautiful treasure in the middle of May! We make our way in that direction, avoiding the dry path to the right of the snowy valley. We want to make sure that we walk straight through the snow. I feel like a kid again. Something as simple as snow now takes on a beautiful new characteristic. It will come to represent for me what we will see throughout this trip: hidden treasures found only through getting lost.

Upon arriving at the top of the hill past the snow, we see a town! We still haven't seen a marker but we figure that this is the right track. Sure enough, it is a town (albeit a small one) named Busdongo, and we pick up a marker and are on our way again. All those hills and getting lost remind me of a valuable lesson I learned on my first Camino many years ago. I can't stress out when I get lost on the trail and can't seem to find my way. I have to be patient and go over that next hill. It is by getting lost that we many times find the true beauty on the Camino.

It is metaphorical to the life lesson that the Camino teaches all who walk it. It is a lesson that we should apply to our daily lives when we have left the trail behind. We have to get lost sometimes to truly find ourselves. The search for that perfect American dream will many times lead us into a false sense of identity. Speaking from personal experience, I am different from what I was when I first walked the Camino as a freshman in college many years ago. I look back and remember how I thought the Camino would change my life and change the way I lived my daily life back home. It did: for a while. I soon got busy with school, extracurricular activities, and jobs, and I forgot the life-changing power the Camino has. I eventually entered graduate school and accumulated more bills. I was losing touch with who I really was.

When the opportunity to participate in this trip arose, I jumped at the chance. I realize now, more than ever, the importance of not just "doing" the Camino but letting the Camino seep into every aspect of your being. You have to lose yourself in it to be able to find out who you really are. This all sounds so abstract and vague but for those of you who have walked it, I need say no more. There is nothing like waking up at six or seven in the morning and sharing a meager breakfast with complete strangers (who will probably become lifelong friends) and starting your daily trek. You have no plans. You have no itinerary. It's just you and the trail.

So, after having gotten "lost," I realize all these things and cannot wait to get lost again to see what other hidden gem I can find. I put lost in quotation marks because in reality you are never really lost. You are merely taking a much-needed detour. You and the Camino have become one. You carry a little bit of it with you wherever you go in life. Sometimes you may forget the lessons it teaches you, but the Camino never leaves you. It is just waiting for the right moment, the right hill, to remind you that you are not alone, that you are not lost, that there is more to this life than you think. So, when you think you are lost, whether it be on the trail or in your daily life, remember that you can never really get lost when you have never even left the trail. *Buen Camino.*

EL CAMINO: A COMMUNAL STORY

Tal Jacobs

We sleep just above the banks of the river that years ago swallowed the streets of old Portomarín, its remnants still protruding from the shallows. The site is mysterious and remote, perfect for igniting the imagination and magnifying the sounds of the night. The plan is simple, the trap set, and the target slumbering. I smoothly pull the line, drawing it through the window and over the roof where it snakes its mischievous path. It sings as it moves intently through the night air. I let the line glide down; dropping it to a thud — crackle, crackle! A mellow cacophony disturbs the still of dark. We wait: nothing. Again, I draw up the line, it groans as it moves across the tin roof, and... release. Our quarry cannot resist. We hear the girls' voices in their cabin. Lights flicker on and off. We continue the ruse until our friends move onto the porch where they look out toward the river for signs of life. But our trap is safe, undetectable with the fishing line arched over the roof and into our window, cleverly suspending a bottle of rocks above the sleeping *peregrinas*.

The next morning we woke early to a sharp knock from a member of our fellowship. She had circles of sleeplessness round her eyes and a tangled assembly of line and bottle in hand. "I believe this is yours?" she asked with drawn-out contempt. Our ploy worked better than expected. Underneath a dark sky and foggy river that concealed a buried town, all we needed was the power of suggestion. The imagination of our friends created an experience, a story so provoking that it came to life.

On the Camino de Santiago, the stories we learned and experienced became as real as the events and characters that shaped them. This is the essence of the Camino. It is myth, legend, and story. Its history, oral tradition, and people carry a shared spiritual identity. They brought me into a unifying collection of movement and effort — the community of pilgrimage. The Camino is a mosaic of people and their experiences from across the world and time. Each pilgrim brings a personal history and his piece of the globe.

We set out — nine students and two professors on course to experience the Camino de Santiago. But our Camino did not begin upon arrival in Spain. It started where any pilgrimage should, at our home, which is Washington and Lee University. We spent three weeks on campus to prepare for our trip and learn the rich history of the Camino while studying what we would encounter. Our investigations covered the tumultuous record of the Iberian Peninsula, the Moorish occupation, and the discovery of St. James' tomb at Campus Stellae. We learned about the Christian reconquest and reclamation of Spain, the birth of a Spanish national identity, and how these shaped the early history of the Camino. The famous literature surrounding the birth of the Camino provided our primary context. We read *The Song of Roland,* and most importantly, Aymeric Picaud's *Codex Calixtinus.* The first travel guide ever written, the *Codex* contains early descriptions of the people and customs of the Camino as well as the earliest liturgy. It gave us some of our first views of the individual places and kinds of people who would be on the pilgrimage, and although the French author's perspective is quite dramatized, many of its insights hold true even today. However, the Navarrese people are much more civil in regard to their animals than Picaud claims (those who have read the *Codex* know what I mean).

Though difficult for a freshman to admit, a coursework setting can provide the most rewarding lens of investigation. Academic study reveals the intricacies one would not ordinarily consider. Neither convenient nor easy, education is supposed to hurt a little bit. Every pilgrim knows this concept of pushing past the pain. When you invest sweat and toil, put your heart and soul into something, you cannot help but appreciate small gifts along the way.

Our coursework primed my palate for learning about the culture and essence of the Camino. As I walked, the places reminded me of the tales I first heard half a world away. The stories of the trail — their allusions, details, and plot twists — became clearer on the journey.

On campus I completed a research paper on Hospital de Órbigo, a small town that connects the path between the gleaming cities of León and Astorga. It hosts a bridge called El Passo Honrosso, built by the Romans for the silver trade, partially destroyed to slow the pursuit of Napoleon's army, and named for one of the most emblematic stories of the Camino.

It was the summer of 1434 when a courageous *caballero* by the name of Don Suero de Quiñones and his supporting knights came to Órbigo with a challenge. Don Suero arrived under captivity of a woman's love, wearing an iron collar to symbolize his imprisonment. He pledged to defeat all comers at a tournament. Don Suero said that he would not rest until he and his men broke 300 lances upon the challengers. He fell only once, and in the spirit of the persevering pilgrim, recovered and said, "It is nothing!" Don Suero's dominance was such that one of his challengers wore two suits of armor for their dual. Quiñones, meanwhile, donned a woman's linens in playful display of his infallibility. The knights prevailed, and Don Suero shed his iron shackle. Upon completing their feat of gentility and knightly worth, Don Suero and his men completed the pilgrimage to finalize their reputations of valor. The story epitomizes the ideal of the *caballero del Camino*, the gentleman knight and champion of the trail. The bridge over the river Órbigo was named El Passo Honrosso to honor the gallantry of the tournament and the men who jousted before the bridge. In their spirit, the competition is replayed each summer, and the winner is named *el mantenedor*, or steward of the bridge.

As I cross the bridge into Órbigo, I enter the world of Don Suero. The troubadour bows before me, and with a blow of his horn, announces my arrival to the growing crowd. I see the banners waving, the horses run in the field beneath the bridge. Along the river stand the wind-craned poplar trees and men fishing the waters for its famous trout. There is a mystical quality to the moment as I enter Don Suero's tournament. I am part of the history of the Camino, filled with the emotion of countless pilgrims before and after me. And as I stand on the bridge and tell my friends this tale, I feel myself become part of the story, in rhythm with the Camino.

When we settled for lunch, I was teeming with the emotion of the town and the tournament. As the shopkeeper wiped glasses at the bar, I approached and asked him about the town's history. Born in Órbigo, he had completed the Camino several times. He pointed me to his *Compostelas* on the wall, hanging alongside a picture of his friend dressed as St. James with staff and cloak. They were medals of a real champion. He gave me a poster from the annual tournament and signed it. To me this was as good as parchment from Don Suero's hands. This man before me had the swagger and stewardship of *el mantenedor*. Living in service and with the fiery heart of competition, he was a *hospitalero* with a warm meal waiting for every *peregrino* who crossed his bridge.

I believe life is about seizing the story. If you want to befriend a person, really know him, and look into his soul, then the purest way is to listen to his story. My professors prepared me to ask the right questions so I could understand the Camino's legend. From there, I immersed myself in the culture and tales of the Camino. But sometimes the story captures you as one of its own. You no longer seek purpose; you are unexpectedly and uncontrollably infused with purpose. It was in these awe-filled moments that I appreciated my role and understood what life was about — there in the moment.

One of those moments seized me while I sat in an internet café in Astorga. It had been a long but rewarding day. Earlier, I had passed through a small town when church bells began to ring and a crowd spilled from its portico onto the street.

The bells could be heard for miles and sang for a solid hour. As I was walking the hill up to Astorga, I saw another string of people carrying some sort of relic. I stopped and asked what was going on: it was the procession of San Isidro. I still didn't understand; I was just really tired and ready to find the *albergue*. Later that day, we visited the Roman ruins hidden in the basements of Astorga, visited the Museo del Chocolate, and attempted to enter the cathedral, which unfortunately was closed. Now sitting in the café, I saw my professor Flor come bustling around the corner. She says in her funny accent, "Tal, Tal! 'Com' quickly. You have to come now. It's the *procesión!*"

"Now?" I ask, puzzled.

"Yes," she said, "come, come." I am on the heels of my professor, inexplicably weaving in and out of narrow corners and alleys in a land far from home. The street suddenly opens up into the Gran Plaza, greeting us with a burst of color and people. Tremendous flags of every hue wave high in the air, tree-sized poles balance atop chins and belts, some with people perched halfway up, hanging on merrily. It is an awesome sight: the culmination of the procession of San Isidro. Each flag represents a neighborhood from the countryside and is surrounded by a band of friends nominated to carry the village standard. I have rarely seen or felt such collective display of regional pride. The people clap, dance, and sing in their tradition, keeping a Middle Ages rite in a new millennium.

Flor shouts at me to follow, and I run behind her, threading through hundreds of people. I feel very foreign, a tall, white, blonde American, but also a part of it all. I dash through the streets as a child, without reservation. We are now part of the procession, joined under the oldest and most colorful flag of all — the standard of Vallevieja. A man hands me his wineskin and I drink, not as a stranger from far away, but as a member of his community, as a fellow pilgrim. We proceed past the palace to the front of the cathedral, its doors now open, a warm glow emanating from within.

The Camino, instead of waiting that I might knock at the door to meet it, invites me in as its guest. With a seat at the table, I become part of the party. At that moment, I soak up

173

everything my gut and senses tell me. I need no rationale to drop my jaw in awe and wonder. I am part of something bigger: a real community. I do not have to try to live, I am absorbed into the vitality of the Camino; and that is living.

I felt a similar sentiment in the forests of Galicia and Samos. The town of Samos possesses a rich but elusive history. It is home to the oldest monastery in Spain, founded in the sixth century. It was the intellectual nucleus of the region and housed one of the great libraries of the ancient world, storing the knowledge and chronicles of Galicia. Centuries ago the monastery burned, leaving only a door, a cornerstone, and a cross. Although the structure has been rebuilt, the written history of Galicia was lost in the fire, shrouding the region in mystery. With a landscape more reminiscent of Scotland or Ireland than the rest of Spain, Galicia teems with Celtic tradition and lore of witchcraft. The regional drink, called the *queimada*, is an absinthe brewed in a cauldron and lit aflame. The local dialect is *Gallego*, a guttural, rough speech to match its coarse, stout people. Galicia challenges every prior conception I had of Spain.

Soon after leaving the town of Samos, I find myself walking through a forest of intense greens and thick trees. The air is heavy here. I am enveloped in old wisdom and frightening stillness. Winding the eerie trails, I meet strange creatures — fallen trees with trunks like the bodies of mighty animals, frozen in wood. I encounter a black squirrel, and later in Galicia, a horse — just as black — standing half hidden in a shady grove of trees. It is as if I walked into a set from *The Lord of the Rings*. I envision that Tom Bombadil or some fantastic sprite might next amble out of a quiet spring or slide down a tree. The air buzzes silently with activity. Shivers fly down my spine. I feel I am being watched out here alone on the trail. Though afraid, I also feel a sense of comfort, not because I am safe, but because I feel alive. The wildness and ancient wisdom grasp me in fear and awe. Here is a presence bigger than myself that makes me embrace my small role, in synchrony with nature and the forces controlling it. God is the only refuge in this land, but I think that He wants me to feel exposed. That is what the Camino is: a heightened sense of being, an aliveness that comes with the realization of vulnerability.

The story of Galicia is written in the rings of the trees, felt in its gnarled roots. It can be smelled in the heavy musk of the woods, like a library of books moistened with the perspiration of the ages. But the wildness of Galicia is not like that of America. There are no sharp crags or rocky mountains or untamed, fierce lands. It has been inhabited, experienced, and shaped. It has a story to tell, albeit a weighty one wrought with emotion. To capture it is like catching smoke. Rather, it must be swallowed whole.

The Camino sucked me in, made me a part of it. I was an actor in its tale. The author placed me where I needed to be. It seemed like every fork in the road I chose, every decision I made, and every person I met was the right one. Despite the best efforts of the yellow arrows and scallop shells to guide the way, I once encountered a series of unlabeled intersections that threatened to lead me astray. Yet for each one, I simply followed my feet. By the fourth junction, my intuition gave me confidence in my choices. I didn't know the facts, I just understood. I was no longer walking on the Camino, but with it. It became my companion, guiding as we spoke in stepwise exchange. I was able to become part of its story because I put myself on the path. I put my faith on the line like those before me, and I was carried forward. I grew to have faith in the story, not worrying about the identity or intent of my character. I simply trusted my action.

On the Camino, the doing defines direction. Instinctual and metaphysical senses sharpen. The cadence of stride calms the mind and tames logic. The beat of my feet finds a rhythm that courses along different textures, stops, and starts to create a symphony — hitting a natural resonance with which life moves at the proper pace. Its progress does not slow for boredom. It floats along with the flowing energy of the day, of other pilgrims, of rest, wine, and song. In grounded movement I sense exactly my place in the world. Connected with the feet of every other pilgrim, I am here, in the only place I need to be. The Camino thrust me into its heart. I had to reach out and embrace it, often without understanding or even feeling the need to do so.

My final project in the course pressed me to reflect on my experience — to relive its emotion and drama but also to discern the subtleties behind its moving power. The Camino is told through images and icons. It is a tale reinforced by repetition and familiarity. I found comfort in the sight of St. James bearing his staff and gourd. My feet gained traction in *la vieira*, the emblematic scallop shell lining the path. It is the captured imagination of all pilgrims where these sights take root and a common legacy lives, binding our souls in pain, triumph, and adventure of past and future. For my project, I painted the images that stood out to me most vividly. I tried to express onto paper the emotions I had felt in their presence. The calm valor of El Passo Honrosso reflects into the cool blue of the Rio Órbigo. A lively wisdom dwells in the tangled forest of Galicia, where a path bends into the darkness and out of sight. The mottled brushstrokes mimic the humming stillness in the trees. My paintings are ports of entry into this world. Just as the Camino's imagery recites its descriptive tales, my paintings reconnect me to the story of the Camino. In them I see where the Camino has taken me, how I belong in its saga. The story grows and follows me as I go, but to be crafted into a new chapter, I will have to return.

ON THE SAME ROAD

Cory O'Brien

I walked the Camino in winter. Not a lot of people do it, because it's not smart. It's cold and damp, and food and shelter are scarce. Add the fact that I was flat broke for the duration of my trip, and I struggle now to justify my decision. During the month I spent walking from Pamplona to Finisterre, I met no more than twenty other pilgrims. I will never forget those twenty, but of that group only two are actually burned into my memory. When people asked me about them, I used to say that one was an angel and the other a devil. I'm not sure about that anymore.

Joel was the devil. He was sitting in a bar making a leather tobacco pouch when I met him. Everything about the guy was green. It wasn't me who noticed it, actually. The angel, Dante, pointed it out to me later. Joel wore a grey-green army surplus jacket, and carried a matching backpack. On hot days, he draped the jacket over the backpack, like a scarecrow. His pants and hat weren't green, and his perfectly pointed goatee was grey, so the outfit wasn't complete, but the hat and jacket, combined with his tendency to be found lounging beneath roadside trees, gave enough of an impression.

He started talking to me the moment I walked into the bar, switched from Spanish to English a few sentences in. He spoke English with an Irish accent, and Spanish with an Italian one. He was French. Within five minutes he was asking if I could spare some change for a drink.

As I said, I was flat broke, but there was no shortage of people to buy Joel food and drink, and he sipped wine and smoked hand-rolled cigarettes late into the night. I sat with a German guy named Lucas, around my age. and we listened in awe to Joel's stories. This was his fourth time on the Camino, his third time doing it without money. One of those times, he said, he had just been diagnosed with liver cancer.

"And I said, 'Fuck it, I don't want this,' and I went on the Camino." Joel's two favorite phrases were "Fuck it" and "Yee-haw," and he delivered both in exactly the same tone, smiling wryly like he was about to jump off a bridge. He didn't look like a man who had liver cancer. He told me the Camino had cured him, and I believed him.

I hardly slept that night and crawled out of bed early the next morning to follow him. I'd spent my time up to that point in the company of people who all but sprinted to the next *albergue* each day, and — even worse! — people who would sometimes send their backpacks ahead of them in a van. In Joel I saw something deeper, something true and original. Unfortunately for me, though I woke up in the wee hours, Joel didn't get going until ten or eleven.

I had the good fortune to run into Joel on one of the few occasions he happened to have money, and I soon understood why he so rarely had it. Before the day was out, he had bought two bottles of wine, two pouches of tobacco, and assorted foodstuffs, and had consumed most of it by midday, paying special attention to the tobacco. He shared the wine generously, and never stopped offering me cigarettes no matter how often I declined. I was soon drunk, stumbling through the fields under a heavy backpack, discussing philosophy.

Joel was an anarchist and an atheist. He'd been homeless in more places than I'd even seen. He foraged for magic mushrooms by the roadside, and had two hits of acid hidden at the bottom of his backpack. He explained at length how the Catholics and the capitalists had stolen the Camino, which had originally been aligned along a pagan ley line. All the trails, he explained, were perversions of the path, motivated by agricultural and commercial interests. In the summer he used the stars to navigate, ignoring the marked trail.

It quickly became clear to me that Joel didn't want a traveling companion. He was happy to teach me the tricks of walking the Camino penniless; asking for day-old bread at the *panaderias*, finding places to stay for free, etc., but he moved at an irregular pace that he kept regardless of those around him. He walked briskly, without seeming to expend any effort at all, easily leaving younger pilgrims trudging along in his wake. On the other hand, he took frequent cigarette breaks, saying to me many times, "If I'm not walking, I'm smoking." I lost him again and again on the trail, only to find him sitting in the shade by the roadside, working on a cigarette or two. In my two days with him I inhaled enough second-hand smoke to make me consider taking up the habit.

The last night I spent with Joel was in Logroño. We stood out on the balcony of an *albergue* where the *hospitalero* had granted both of us a free stay. He smoked a cigarette, and I stood shivering and listening to him talk. I'd told him that I was looking for the right way to do the Camino, that I thought he represented that.

"Find your own Camino," he said. "You can't walk someone else's. The first time I did the Camino, I was about your age. I walked 70 kilometers a day. This was the Camino del Norte, too. Up and down mountains, brutal on the knees. I ended up in a hospital, tendonitis. They told me I couldn't walk for a week, and I *cried*. I just wanted to be walking. So, you can walk 70 kilometers per day. I did it. But *hombre* ... go at your own pace. Some days you may only walk to the next town, find a place to stay, and fuck it. Walk faster than people. Lose them. Meet them a week later. You're all on the same road."

He was right, too. Everyone I met on the Camino I lost and met again in Santiago. Everyone except for Joel. Joel and Dante.

I knew about Dante long before I actually met him. Whenever anyone found out I was from California, they'd ask if I was a friend of his. One day, I asked Joel if he'd met him.

"Oh, Dante. Very religious guy. He has a little bit of a prophet complex. Very preachy. Little bit off in the head. When I arrived at the *albergue* where I met him, I heard him arguing with the *hospitalero*. All I heard was the *hospitalero*. He said, 'I'll let you stay tonight, but you better not try what you tried yesterday.' During dinner he was sharpening the *albergue*'s knives. That was how he paid his way."

I wanted to find Dante owing to equal parts homesickness and curiosity. The number of enigmas in Joel's descriptions only increased my desire to meet the man. What had he done to upset the *hospitalero*? Why did he sharpen knives? Was he a murderer? Did he have magical powers?

I was so intent on meeting Dante that I created a self-imposed walking schedule intended to close the apparent two-day gap between him and me. Like all my attempts at self-imposed walking schedules, this one was poorly planned and overly ambitious, and I ended up a sore mess in an *albergue* 10 miles closer than I'd planned to be by the end of the day, lying in bed and complaining of my failure to Lucas.

That was when Dante walked into the room. When I explained the situation to him, he only looked at the ceiling with a slight smile and said, "God knows."

Dante was roughly the same age as Joel, 45. His black-and-grey beard created a massive square jawline beneath his chin. He sported a bowl cut and pale blue eyes, and always seemed to speak from some ways away. No sooner had I met him than I started asking questions. He was happy to answer.

He had been on a pilgrimage for ten years, not two, but had not actually walked across the United States. He had hitchhiked to a number of places after selling all his worldly possessions, and had spent several years with his "spiritual family" in Mexico.

He showed me a duct-taped together day planner, with a world map glued inside the front cover. His route was traced in red pen. He'd been to London, Jerusalem, and all over North and Central America. As he continued to talk, I flipped through the planner itself, which seemed to serve as an abbreviated journal. All I got to see before he took the book back was: "I saw darkness at the bottom of stairs."

That creeped me out. Meanwhile, Dante was explaining to me why he had become a pilgrim. His troubles had begun more than sixteen years before, when a one-night stand with a fellow church member led to an unplanned pregnancy. He and his lover agreed to keep the child, but as their relationship wore on, Dante began to see his wife as a manipulator and not enough of a Christian. "She was using my son, Austin, to control me." And yet he stayed. He stayed and tried to keep his family together. He tried for years, until he received a message from God telling him to move on, to leave his wife and child. So he did.

He began seeking work as a hair stylist, his lifelong trade. He was living with his mother, struggling to make a living, feeling desperate and lost. One night, sitting on the floor in his room, Dante cried out to God, screamed for mercy. He felt a change in himself, a new kind of energy. God spoke to him, he said, in a clear, calm voice and told him to open his Bible. It fell open to a page describing a prophet undergoing the very experience he was having. He read verse after verse, and felt he understood each of them as never before. The most vivid detail in his story, the one thing he was very clear on, was that he did not need to blink. He read and prayed for hours, but did not blink.

He fell asleep and dreamt with great clarity of awakening in a bedroom with a vivid painting of a golden rose hanging over the bed. No more than a month later, a female friend of his offered him an apartment to live in. When he entered the bedroom, he stopped and began to cry. Hanging over the bed was the very same painting from his dream. His faith was affirmed.

Not long after these events, God told Dante to sell his possessions and become a pilgrim. In his head Dante had a much different definition of the word "pilgrim" than anyone else I met on the Camino.

"A pilgrim," he told me, standing in front of my bunk bed as I leafed through his planner, "is someone who is walking, waiting for the kingdom of God." To Dante, a pilgrimage had no endpoint. A pilgrimage was a way to pass the time 'til judgment day.

He did indeed sharpen knives, as Joel had warned me. It was a holdover from his days as a freelance hairdresser, when he used to sell his services to barbershops, sharpening scissors. That was how he paid his way at the *albergue* where we both stayed. I paid my way by washing dishes. One day, out of curiosity, I asked Dante if he remembered Joel. He told me that he had met him one night in an *albergue,* but that Joel had been too drunk to get to know. It sounded to me as if he knew Joel pretty well.

Despite his many years of living in Mexico, Dante's Spanish was terrible. He spoke with a thick California accent, and so slowly that he seemed almost to be condescending to his listeners.

He had invented his own sect of Christianity more or less. As he explained to every *hospitalero* who offered him pork or asked him to leave the *albergue* on a Saturday morning, *"Soy judeo-cristiano.* I am Judeo-Christian." He obeyed Jewish law, especially dietary restrictions, while accepting Jesus Christ as his personal savior. His laws often prevented him from eating with the rest of us.

First of all, he would not eat until God told him he could. He would sometimes fast for a day or two because he had not been given permission to eat. When he did eat, he usually could not share in whatever the other pilgrims made because he did not eat pork (which ruled out most of the meat we had on us) or even tuna (apparently because it is an animal without scales.). I learned most of this on Christmas Eve, when a fellow pilgrim and I prepared a special dinner. Our Christmas dinner was fragmented, with me and a jolly young Hungarian named Attila sharing a tuna and cheese salad while Dante ate bread and honey. Before the meal, Dante suggested a prayer to God, thanking him for the food. Attila and I, both atheists, but good-natured atheists, agreed. What followed was an impromptu sermon on the grace of God and Jesus Christ, dissolving into repetition, lasting twenty minutes or more. Every other sentence was punctuated with, "You are so GOOD, God. You are SO GOOD." As if he were eating a delicious sandwich composed of the Lord.

Though I traveled with Dante for three days, we never actually walked together. In fact, the reason Dante and I ended up in the same *albergue* in the first place was that he was unable to walk any farther. This was, I think, mainly due to poor planning. He carried not only a full backpack, but also a handcart loaded with more of his worldly possessions. I struggled along the Camino wearing a single 20-pound pack and arrived in Santiago with a hip injury that still bothers me when the weather changes. I shudder to imagine what Dante was doing to himself dragging that handcart over mountains, through the snow.

But thankfully for him, this was a sign from God. A sign that he was to spread the word among the pilgrims, that one did not need to actually *walk* the Camino in order to be a pilgrim. God wanted pilgrims to swallow their pride, to accept rides from passing strangers instead of stoically rejecting them as I had done more than once. He had a point. The longer I walked, the more people told me that it was the *attitude* and *intent* that made a pilgrim, not the method of transport. Certainly, you are likely to find more tourists than hardened pilgrims taking the bus, but if a pilgrim is only passing time waiting for the kingdom of heaven, what does it matter how fast he travels or who he travels with?

Though I didn't believe in the same things Dante did, I had to admit that God had yet to lead him wrong. The night we met, Dante was impressed by the fact that I was walking the Camino without any money, with only a backpack. He said that my faith restored his own, and he thanked me so much I was embarrassed. That night, after mumbling his evening prayers, Dante called me over to his bunk.

"God wants me to give you this," he said, and handed me a ten euro note. Ten euros was a fortune to me at that time. Ten euros meant five days, maybe even a week's worth, of food. It meant I could pay for a bed one night instead of begging. I felt horrible taking money from this injured pilgrim, especially since it was clear to me that he was insane. I tried to refuse, but he insisted. Let me tell you, it is very hard to turn down a gift from God.

The next day, when my shoes rubbed my ankles raw, filled with ice water, and forced me to walk barefoot to the general store that evening, it was Dante who found me new shoes. He asked the proprietor of a nearby bar if he had any sons, and if those sons had any extra shoes. And the next day I had a new pair of shoes. They were beat up, and they weren't waterproof, but they fit, thank the Lord. Thus God granted me yet another gift through Dante.

I feel bad even now, because despite my misgivings about Dante, he seemed convinced that God wanted him to walk with me. I think he wanted to convert me. He never did, but I did do something for him. The last night we stayed together, on Christmas Eve, he asked if I would deliver a message to his son when I got back to California. He wrote the contact information in my waterlogged address book, and the next morning I left the *albergue* and never saw him again. He didn't plan on walking. It was a Saturday. He was arguing in his awful Spanish with the *hospitalero* when I left. So it goes.

It took me a long time after getting home to call Dante's son. One reason was that I actually forgot my address book in Spain and had to have it mailed to me via London. The other reason was that I was worried. I wasn't sure what to say to the son Dante had abandoned more than 10 years ago.

I have to amend an earlier statement. God had led Dante wrong. God had led Dante to leave his family, to leave his child. After two months of putting off the promised telephone call, I dialed Austin — Dante's son. His mom, Linda, picked up. We spoke for over an hour about Dante, about who he was when she fell in love with him, about who he had become by the time he left her. She said she knew Dante loved his son. He had cried when he held newborn Austin in his arms. But he soon began to impose bizarre restrictions on the boy. For one thing, he wouldn't let his son play with toys, as he said it amounted to idolatry. He objected to underwear with cartoon characters on it for the same reason. At one point, Linda told me, he actually took all the offending undergarments and cut out their logos. He stuffed the scraps into a plastic garbage bag and carried them out of the house.

As for Austin, he didn't even want to talk to me. He did talk, though only for a minute. I tried to apologize for what his father had done to him. He told me it was old news. He told me I should go. I didn't know what else to say. I wasn't on the Camino anymore. There weren't any yellow arrows to tell me how to comfort an estranged son. I told him his father was alive and somewhat healthy, and let him give the phone back to his mother.

In two weeks, I'm going down to Los Angeles. I'm planning to meet Linda and Austin in Orange County where they live. Maybe I'll have something to say to Austin by then. Maybe I'm still on the path. Maybe this is the next stop. At the beginning of this story I said I wasn't sure if my angel-devil opposition stood up. It doesn't. If Joel was a Devil, he was a generous devil with decades of wine-drunk wisdom to share. A devil in retirement, at worst. If Dante was an Angel, he was an angel who walked out on his infant son, who left his wife to raise the child alone. A fallen angel at best. So really, sitting at my desk with the benefit of hindsight and journal entries, I can't cast them as the divinities that my storyteller's sensibilities demand. I can't even be sure I won't meet them again.

After all, we're all on the same road.

LETTER TO A PROFESSOR

Christian Man

For Nick Barker
IN MEMORIAM
1937-2009

Dear Dr. Barker:

Today was the first in October. It was my niece's second birthday — her name is Jane. We went and ate cookies at a café, and afterwards we went into the zoo and looked at the animals. Near the pelicans, there is a golden patch of pin oaks under which we walked, with Jane on the shoulders of her mother, Lily, and the waning strength of light in the gloaming. Looking up, I thought of John Muir in his Yosemite Valley, and how his trees were *psalm-singing*. I thought of your back porch.

Do you remember, once, when you wrote a poem you called "Contrition"? It only said: "I / regret / words." I hope this letter doesn't remind you of that poem, even though, as I write, I am reminded of it. I want to tell you about a walk I took one spring, and I want the steps themselves to be like a cadence, or maybe a psalm, replacing the words that limit me. Honestly, I want you to be proud of me.

* * *

They were strangers and exiles on the earth. That is from a letter whose author we do not know. Some people think about that verse in terms of pilgrimage, but when I think about that old practice, I envision a cedar tree. The Camino de Santiago, for all its forests and trees and saplings, has no such cedars. It probably never will. Those trees grow in Lebanon, and it is the

191

Psalmist who speaks of them; he says that the righteous *grow like a cedar in Lebanon.* I want to tell you more about that.

* * *

From the outset, the way of St. James was unambiguous in what it asked of us. We started in Le Puy-en-Velay on a cloudy Thursday morning with toast and black tea, then mass in a stone chapel, then communion, where we prayed at length, kneeling, asking for sustenance. The body of Christ, *broken for us.* My friend Douglas and I stepped through the cathedral's threshold lockstep, in jackets, without a sound but the scraping of the snow beneath our feet.

Lunch that day was basic. Our conversation was an attempt to reframe what we immediately accepted as a bad decision: 1,500 kilometers of lonely gravel roads. In our orange tent the next night, I lay on my side, frozen, wondering what my family was doing. After a while, the air went out of my sleeping pad. I re-inflated it sleepily, conjuring symbolism and pulling on another pair of socks. Douglas was motionless, and through the trees the constellations, turning imperceptibly, were also silent.

I still think about that. Because sensory perception is anterior to cognitive perception and the categories we place on the world, it seems that the most important moments start when we relent in our obsession with premature understanding and mystery-solving. To want to understand the *notion* behind the observation is to undo our humanness, or at least to try and skip over it.

In other words, this path along which we walked would force us to make peace with our flesh, even if it was an uneasy one. Though pilgrimage is a spiritual and historical practice, it is essentially an *act*. From moment to moment, the act is devoid not of significance but of a *sense* of significance; in the present tense, the themes are not transcendent, but quite literally pedestrian. Eliot was right:

> In order to arrive at what you do not know
> You must go by a way which is the way of ignorance.

In order to possess what you do not possess
    You must go by the way of dispossession.
In order to arrive at what you are not
    You must go through the way in which you are not.
                  (T.S. Eliot, *Four Quartets*)

This was a first lesson: a willful existentialism. There was nothing to rush or change or go beyond. There was a day of walking, bookended by days of walking. On the normal ones, we would finish by four o'clock in the afternoon. We would look for a café or put on our sandals and cook pasta over our small stove. The best thing we found in France was small jars of pesto — the store brand, but very good with spaghetti and fresh tomatoes, which we would slice and salt. After washing the dishes, we might write in our journals as the night came on. At that time I was reading a book by Sherwood Anderson, and my fatigue made me vulnerable to the force of his characters' words. *You must shut your ears to the roaring of the voices,* one of them said.

And I did — we both did. Near the end of the first week, Douglas and I found our rhythm, and it would stay with us, more or less, until we arrived at the base of the Pyrenees in St. Jean Pied de Port nearly four weeks later. The secret was to whistle. We whistled while we worked, so to speak — as Augustine suggested, we "sang, but kept going," greeting uphill climbs with a song of our own making (with a little help from Johnny Appleseed):

> *I see Masseur Colline*
> *It sure looks high to me*
> *So blaze by blaze, and bite by bite*
> *I found that it is out of sight;*
> *I ate Masseur Colline.*

I must tell you that, on the Camino, we laughed to an almost unceremonious degree. I remember one day that had been quite miserable. We had passed through kilometers of thick mud, a dirty industrial town, and beyond that gray shadows of hills that had been viciously strip-mined. At 6:30

p.m. or so, we finally found a stretch of flat ground that looked suitable for our tent. All we had to do was get over the barb-wire fence, which was against our self-imposed good pilgrim policy. Reluctantly, we decided to approach the adjoining farmhouse and ask for permission to sleep on the farmer's land. As we walked into the courtyard (which I use liberally, as there was nothing regal of which to speak), Old McDonald's theater of the absurd commenced. Dogs — rabid, ravenous, foaming — yelped and growled from every corner. Pigs squealed in furious point-counterpoint. From within a hollow grain silo about fifteen feet tall, an indiscernible groan sounded — think *The Sandlot*. Then, as if to formalize this moment of disbelief as we stood there, hiking poles in hand, a blue rooster strutted in proud, perfect form from stage left to stage right, clucking loudly and with such duty. It was as if John Cage had become a zoologist and was doing his practicum.

Backing out slowly so as to keep the mammalian peace, we turned and bent double in the type of laughter that aches deep in your gut. We howled until our eyes were wet. *"Did you see?"* It was no use. We were nodding and weeping and pointing, both at the same time. In that simple cathartic moment, there were no industrial towns. There were no awful strip mines. There was only the blue rooster.

Those are sacred moments, Dr. Barker. In them, God is at a kind of work that is profound and subtle — consecrating, blessing, and healing. For Chesterton this was the Christian's "gigantic secret":

> There was one thing that was too great for God to show us when he walked upon our earth; and I have sometimes fancied that it was his mirth.
>
> (*Orthodoxy*)

Stumbling along the Camino, time and time again, we found ourselves in the freedom of that greatness, and it was, among other things, a catalyst.

* * *

I think that is what first drew me to the trees, as well. They were catalysts, because they bore the trail blazes which we followed: they were how we walked the right way, signs for — and even of — the perseverant. Though often impressive in form, you would come to see the trees' strength in terms of time, not space, for while moving among them — head leaned back — you would come to think of how much and how many they had outlasted. Their patient stature evoked a reverence because of what it signified, like the wrinkles of a king.

Now, trees belong to ecosystems, and before it is anything else, the Camino is an ecological experience. Though the land would come to act as a metaphor for us, it was also a medium, always rewarding in proportion to that which it exacted. One morning, we had risen early, refreshed after the previous day of rest, but were waylaid in our departing by heavy rain. I sat shoeless at the small, comfortable kitchen table of our hostel and drank Verveine tea, drumming my fingers on the table lazily, watching the old gutters gather the rain into little runnels on the side of the street, like some small poem that did not yet have words for itself.

Added to the psychological difficulty of a late start was the immediate steepness of the hills, then the immediate realization that our packs were as heavy as they had ever been, what with a new supply of lentils, cheese, and chocolate, and full bottles of water. It was a slow, wet, contemplative day, and the sky above us was, fittingly, a monolith of gray cloud cover.

After four hours of plodding along, we trudged into a quiet village, drank two good cups of coffee with a friendly town official, and, after fixing dinner at a hostel, reshouldered our packs for one more hour of walking. We did so in order to make up for the time we had lost that morning. That hour, we passed several rather bleak duck farms and discussed at length the stultifying life of the stock *pâté* duck.

The laughing over, we walked in silence for a few moments. As the light began to change, we found ourselves considering the metaphor of pilgrimage — the impulse came from nowhere, or rather from everywhere. We, as pilgrims, longed to arrive in Santiago de Compostela — our destination — even as we made faithful strides toward it. It was a place we could not yet see, this "far country" (C. S. Lewis, "The Weight of Glory"). Our steps were a sort of progressive realization of that end — and yet so was the conversation. It was as if I suddenly saw the path issuing backward from that final place to which it led: because the place was a place, it was — somehow — also a way, and we felt it in our longing.

Fifteen minutes later, we passed through a small dairy farm, rounded a corner, and immediately stopped short: the setting sun, with slants of gorgeous light, had broken with a suddenness into the valley which fell before us, setting ablaze the soaked green pastureland. Somewhere a tractor hummed rhythmically; an unmended fence tilted in an angle of gentle repose; the "whole earth was at rest and at peace; it broke forth into singing." (Isaiah 14:7).

That night Douglas remarked how the beauty of creation is not a sentiment but a revelation — a gift which is "the grace of the world" into which creatures may come (Wendell Berry, "The Peace of Wild Things"). Ultimately, it seemed, we must come as members of the physical world, because membership confers a reverence that, in turn, confers responsibility, and does not responsibility have everything to do with prosperity? To decimate that which we were given to rule over is to forget that authority over creation is really a form of indebtedness. We can not prosper for very long through destruction; we can not preside if we do not first belong.

* * *

Return to the image of the cedar. In the Scriptures, for C. John Collins, it is one of "permanent vitality." It is an image for the people of God. Speaking of one among these people, the Psalmist writes:

> He is like a tree
> planted by streams of water
> that yields its fruit in its season,
> and its leaf does not wither. (Psalm 1:3)

When the drought or the torrent comes, as it will, the tree submits itself, conquering not by force but by endurance. Pilgrims call each other to such an ethic with an ancient Latin term *ultreia*, literally "to move beyond." In days of physical and mental weakness, one must indeed simply push on — *ultreia*, we would tell each other.

Many days I needed to hear this, but none more than on Easter Sunday. That day we had sped through six miles of the thickest mud in order to make a Catholic mass that was utterly disillusioning in its hollowness. We spent the afternoon dealing with rain, sleet, inhospitable café employees, a vicious dog, and a mediocre dinner. There was little in the way of celebrating the resurrection of Jesus Christ, to be sure. I wanted to be gone, to be at home, to be finished, to be among the familiar and the faithful. On such days, you had to be gritty and get through them; you had to set the bar low and tell yourself that, on those days, lying down in the tent at night was the victory.

Other challenges remained with us. Among the costs of walking more than seventy consecutive days, our four feet incurred the greatest debt. In the first few weeks, Douglas had developed a frightening number of toe and heel blisters. He spent good time every night cleaning and dressing them. I was blister-free. When we entered Galicia, however, three weeks out from Compostela, our fortunes traded places, and deep heel blisters soon emerged on my right foot. Heel blisters are a test of the mind and spirit, for the only thing you can do to address them is to exhibit patience and take medicine. You could spot a pilgrim from a mile off if you look for that old, familiar limp.

* * *

That was the way to Compostela, Dr. Barker. It was piecemeal, and it happened among "confession, tears, and great laughter" (Frederick Buechner, *The Sacred Journey*). It also happened in the company of magnificent people. Tatterdemalion and road-weary, we came together as co-laborers, and our friendships were stripped of formality and protocol. What we found underneath was a solidarity that was simple and strong and beautiful. It reminds me of you, and the day when we were sitting at lunch in the back of the cafeteria. Do you remember? We were against the windows that look out over the mountains. You were talking about truth, but forsook the thought mid-sentence as a great bird rose from the valley floor on exquisite wings. *"Look at that!"* was all you could say, eyes ablaze. We did.

By now your blisters, too, have healed, although you never were one for talking about yourself. But — see? — that's what I've been doing all along.

> There is a day
> When the road neither
> Comes nor goes, and the way
> Is not a way but a place.
> (Wendell Berry)

Yours, Christian

A PHOTOGRAPH AND THE IRON CROSS

Anne Tolene

The morning was misty and damp as the tall iron cross, the *Cruz de Ferro*, came into view atop a large pile of rocks. People have added to this mountain of stones for centuries. They have shed their troubles and addictions, concerns and sins, each one represented by a rock that supports this cross. Each story, like each stone left behind, is different: massive or seemingly insignificant, rough or smooth, solid or crumbling. But instead of a rock, I have brought along a picture of my father and me. He had died nearly a year before. I stood looking at the picture of us for what seemed like an eternity before placing it on the pole of the cross under a piece of string used to hold wildflowers.

My story starts on move-in day, freshman year of college. My mother, father, and a couple of my brothers had come to help me move into my new dorm. Dad and I took the first few boxes from the parking lot, and began to walk to the building. I was so excited.

"Anne, Anne, hang on," my dad said to me as he began to lean over to set the box down. Suddenly he was on the ground. I began to panic, and I called an ambulance as people rushed over to help. The hospital was a blur, and two hours later I was on my way home, without my father. He had suffered a heart attack and passed away. I spent the next week with my family in a mess of tears and decisions. I passed blame around, quietly in my head, until nothing was the same anymore. It was no one's fault, but no one was innocent, especially me.

Families are complicated, and mine is an especially large tangle of complex relationships and baggage. I have four older brothers, one older sister, and one younger brother. Two of my brothers and my sister are married with children. Two of my brothers still lived at home, and soon it would be only one. In less than a week, my home went from being full of noisy people to painfully quiet. I couldn't look at my mother anymore. I didn't know what to say to my brothers. The silence was deafening and everything reminded me of my father. I couldn't stand to be there.

I didn't know how to move forward, so when I returned to school, I threw myself into my studies. I did not try to make new friends; I did not grieve in ways that my family expected. Most importantly, I did not tell anyone what had happened. I treated the matter as taboo. Aside from my roommate and the few people who witnessed the event, no one else at school knew, and I liked it that way. All the people around me were wrapped up in their own first semester of college, and no one really noticed anything unusual.

But I was lonely. All of my spare time was spent in the library, and by the time Fall Break came along I needed to get away. I did not want to go home, so I convinced my brother and my roommate to take a canoe trip with me through my university's outdoor program. I spent four days on the Buffalo River with the fall leaves changing. We slept in the woods and our nights were spent around a campfire. Two important things happened that weekend. I laughed and smiled for the first time in months, and I learned about the Camino. Finally, my mind had something new to focus on. I had something to dream about, something to look forward to. I was ready for a change, and traveling in Spain was going to be an adventure.

I was careful about telling my family, and I did not say anything until the plans were finalized and I was ready to buy a plane ticket. I knew they would think that I was just running away from my troubles. And, in the beginning, maybe that was true. All I knew was that I could not spend my summer at home. As much as I loved my family, being with them was hard. My mom thought so too, and by the end of October she had decided to sell our old house and move to Tennessee to live closer to my older brothers.

As I learned about the Camino, my motivations became more focused. I wanted two things. First, I needed to grieve, and doing that from a distance felt much easier than confronting my grief at home. Second, I wanted to be happy. I wanted to learn to love and trust and be open. I wanted to share what I was feeling inside, to break the walls down, to have someone care that I was hurting.

In May, we began our journey in Roncesvalles. I was part of a rather large group of college students, but making friends did not prove to be as hard as I had worried it would be. While I do come from a large family, most of the last year had been spent alone. Now, every moment was spent with someone. We walked together, ate together, slept in the same room. At the end of the day, I was physically and emotionally exhausted. I am not saying that I was unhappy — the combination of exercise, sunshine, and a little bit of wine did wonders for my outlook on life.

Soon, the walking became an afterthought. I loved talking with the people I had met and becoming friends with people I already knew. Together, we explored old Spanish towns, tried new foods, saw beautiful views, danced, and sang. Suddenly, the world that was my life before seemed so far away. Still, something was missing. I longed for those meaningful conversations with my new friends. I wanted to share all of the things that I was feeling inside, but I was nervous. Would they understand? Even more than that, would they care? I wanted to talk, but I didn't want to cry. This was too beautiful a place for tears.

On top of one of the hills in Belorado was a small set of ruins, a castle that once belonged to the Cid, where the view was spectacular. Most of our group went together to see the castle ruins and then went back to the *albergue* once the sun began to set. Some of us, however, continued on above the ruins to see if the view would be better.

When we reached the top of the steep hill, we found a large field. Without saying a word, we looked at each other and took off running, moving away from the town as the sun set behind us. The wheat stalks slapped swiftly against my legs, and stones hidden from sight hurt my bare feet. But none of that mattered. The field felt endless, and the wind was cool as it blew across my face. Uncontrollable laughter overtook me. Even if I had wanted to, I couldn't have willed myself to stop. Suddenly, I stopped to catch my breath. Two of my friends stood beside me, and we looked out over the field. Standing there, for a moment, I was free and nothing mattered. But things change quickly.

Soon after we arrived in Burgos, I made my first phone call home. I had let my family know I had arrived safely in Spain through an email in Pamplona, but not much else. When I finally talked to my mom, she confirmed all my fears. My family's life was deteriorating at home, full of broken relationships and grief. My family was dealing with the past year, almost as well as I was — badly, or not at all. I was so far away. By the time I got off the phone, I was in tears — not because I was homesick but because I never wanted to go home again.

I was overwhelmed by emotion and just needed to let it out. I talked to the first person I saw, but I didn't know how to explain what I was feeling. It felt too complicated, and I didn't know where to begin. The conversation was short. I don't even think most of what I said made sense. If my own family didn't understand, what made me think someone else would? Nearly as soon as I began talking, I felt an overwhelming urge to escape. I ran.

Instead of talking, I went away by myself and cried all the tears that I had been holding inside for far too long. I cried until there wasn't anything left, and it felt good. Whatever wall that was there keeping me from expressing my emotions had begun to break away.

After that brief conversation, I felt compelled to put on a happy face despite my true emotions. I thought that by acting more cheerful I might come to feel that way. I told myself, "I'm in Spain! There is no need to be sad. All my problems are thousands of miles away."

Then the vast Meseta began, and the group I was walking with split into pairs. Our first day walking went so well. I talked and laughed with my friend. I told her about my dad — in a short-and-sweet "now you know; now we don't have to talk about it anymore" kind of way. While one part of me really wanted to share my story, another part of me just wanted to keep the hurt hidden away so no one would know my suffering. But by now at least I had told the essential details to a friend.

Still, though, my afternoons were filled with lonely thoughts. I cried often now, alone. I wanted to feel again the way I had felt in the field above Belorado, free from pain. Soon, we stopped in Castrojeriz, and again checked into the *albergue*.

A few of us went to explore the castle ruins on the hill that could be seen from the road. Once we arrived at the top, I went exploring and decided to climb up the side of the castle ruins. I fell off, and I took a friend down with me. It hurt, and I felt so thoughtless. I didn't cry walking back down the hill. I wasn't ready to let anyone see me break down, even if this time they could see why.

Walking back down the hill, one of my fellow pilgrims said to me, "If you are too hurt, I will leave my pack and carry you all the way to Santiago." I smiled. I had made friends. When we got back to the *albergue*, my cuts needed to be cleaned and bandaged. When that was done, another friend took me away. We sat on a bench, underneath a tree. I talked. I talked about my family, all of the guilt, regret, and hurt from my father's passing. I just kept talking, answering questions, and listening. I didn't look him in the eyes once, but it felt good to let some of my pain go.

That night, I sat outside talking with my friends. Someone mentioned sleeping atop the castle, and we did. Four of us climbed the hill again and went to the top of the castle tower. With the sun setting, the view was stunning. We laid our sleeping bags out, and looked up at the stars as we feel asleep. We were together, each lost in our own thoughts. That night I made a wish on the first shooting star I had ever seen, and it was magical.

The rest of my days on the Meseta were peaceful, and soon we reached León, the beginning of the third and final part of our journey. In this stage of the Camino, the group split up. I chose not to go with the friends I knew the best but rather with the ones I wanted to get to know better. I wanted these people to help me grow stronger in expressing my emotions without fear. I went with people I knew I could talk to and who would let me make my own decisions.

In this last section of the Camino, I became myself. I said what I thought; I did what I felt. I missed my other friends, but I felt free. This last week on the Camino I was happy, sad, frustrated, hopeful, and upset. In feeling all these emotions and enduring all my problems, I did not hide. I learned to cope. I did what I needed to do to find peace inside.

Not long after, we came upon the Iron Cross, the *Cruz de Ferro*. The morning was foggy. There were people all around me, placing their stones, taking pictures, making noise. It didn't feel spiritual or sacred. It didn't have to. As I secured the picture of my father and me to the large pole supporting the cross, I realized that everyone carries stones inside. Yes, I was broken, but I looked at all of the rocks around me. My friends placed their stones — why didn't I know what they were for? They had not told me their hurt either.

Everyone has pain. Everyone suffers. It is part of life. What made me any different? All of my feelings, the guilt and hurt and grief, were normal. Finally, I felt like it was okay to be upset, to cry. I suddenly didn't have the need to feel strong.

By the last day on the Camino, most of the other group had caught up with us. Arriving in Santiago, I knew my father would have been proud of me. I knew he wanted me to be happy, and maybe, I was ready to feel that way again. I hugged the statue of St. James, marveled at the Cathedral, and acquired my hard-earned *Compostela*. I spent these last few days with my good friends, basking at the beach in the warmth of the sun and our hearts, before we all went our separate ways.

Pilgrims who make their way to the cathedral in Santiago often speak of their journey as a transformational experience, yet the transformation is rarely completed along the route itself. I am still the same person I was before walking to Santiago, just less broken and more open. Along the Way, I learned to grieve, and I began to accept myself and how I feel.

I carried a new perspective away by leaving an old photograph of my father and me, my symbolic rock, atop the Iron Cross.

AFTERWORD:

THE CAMINO IN WINTER

Andrew Talbot Squires

It never snows in Portomarín. We are at too low an elevation," the bar owner smilingly reassured us as she brought two steaming bowls of *caldo gallego,* rich with potatoes and kale floating in a deliciously oily broth. As I sopped up the rest of my soup with the thick yet airy bread typical of Galicia, my mother and I mulled over our trip. What I noticed consistently about walking the Camino in January was the stillness. Four years earlier, she and I had hiked through Portomarín in the summer. The streets were busy with cars and pilgrims in all directions. At 9 p.m., we pilgrims settled into bed as the sun began to set, while the rest of Spain — those who didn't have to wake up at 5:30 a.m. and walk 20 kilometers — lounged at a bar and laughed with friends over glasses of *vino tinto.* Yet tonight, in the depth of winter, the town sat still at 8 p.m., already blanketed in darkness for over two hours. We could see our breath as we walked in silence along the frosty cobblestones.

I had hiked the Camino before — splitting the French route over two summers in high school and walking the Camino Portugués the previous summer — so a trip to return with my mother and hike the 200 kilometers from Sarria to Santiago and on to Muxía did not seem particularly daunting. Yet my mother's suggestion that we hike in January was something I had never contemplated. I remember looking at guidebooks in the 90-degree heat of the Meseta to find a bar in the next few kilometers. Many entries ended with the comment, "May be open only sporadically during the winter months."

Walking through Spain in the darkness and cold of winter and worrying about bars being open seemed almost comical when we sometimes felt like dinosaurs in the scene from Disney's *Fantasia*. Yet the trip fit in perfectly with my college winter break, and I am not one to turn down free trips to Europe.

We returned to our *albergue* that night and greeted the four other pilgrims there. I checked on my slow-cooking socks on the radiator, and, deciding that one side was about medium-well, I flipped them over. A vital part of an enjoyable winter *albergue* stay is the radiator-to-pilgrim ratio. In the summer, washed clothes and wet socks are a slight annoyance easily fixed by a few hours in the bright sun. In the winter, radiators are key. There is always a good-natured yet serious game played between fellow pilgrims at allotting space for draping socks, shirts, and shoes over the radiator. No one wants to hog the entire space with their clothing, yet no one wants to wake up to a 30-degree morning and put on wet shoes and socks. Luckily, we each had a radiator to ourselves, and even copies of the newspaper *La Voz de Galicia*, which I crammed into my shoes and swapped every few hours. The soporific combination of food and stuffy heat soon put me to sleep as I curled up in my sleeping bag.

The winter gives one much more time for three activities — reading, contemplating, and sleeping. As the sun doesn't rise until 8 a.m., there is little point in going to bed before at least 11 p.m., the only problem being how to fill several hours of free time in the cold and dark. I brought a large stack of books I had bought at a used bookstore, so had no hard feelings when I left them as I finished them. My mother shook her head when the weight of my books was greater than the weight of my sleeping bag. So, most evenings I would read for hours, which in turn led me to contemplate how winter changes the pilgrim's perspective. Anyone who steps on the Camino knows how much it simplifies life — you carry nothing more than your pack, and your focus changes from the outward and speculative world of new cell phones, party plans, and worries about tests to the concrete world of injuries and mileage.

In a very real sense, a pilgrim today lives like someone out of the past. Yet the winter underscored this reality for me. I understood more fully why winter foods were hearty and fattening, why winter nights feel like they last forever, and how a warm place is truly a protection from the outside. This speculation extended to walking. The few pilgrims on the road meant we might only see two or three others during a whole day of walking. After my mother and I had exhausted most conversation points in the first three days, we frequently walked in silence, and the landscape reflected and reinforced this withdrawal. The fields, gardens, and trees seemed frozen solid in the mornings, and the stiffness of the world around us encouraged silence. Finally, the winter brought sleeping. On most nights I would head to bed around eleven, not waking up for nine hours, made even easier by the relative lack of pilgrims snoring.

So I awoke around 8 a.m. in the *albergue* at Portomarín and began the routine preparations that every pilgrim makes in the morning — stuffing my sleeping bag, brushing my teeth, filling my water bottle, and packing my pack in the exact order I had memorized. We looked outside, and instead of the cobblestone streets and shingle roofs, the landscape was blanketed in the uniform whiteness of snow. So much for our barkeep's weather predictions, because there certainly was snow in Portomarín.

We headed out of the *albergue*, snow crunching underfoot, and gingerly eased our way down the steep and now-slippery cobblestone street. There were no other footsteps in the snow, no car tracks on the road, and no sounds at all. The normal quiet had been even further stifled by the muffling effect of the snow. As we crossed the bridge over the reservoir, a Guardia Civil car slowly eased its way up the street, its occupants probably shaking their heads in wonder at both the snow and the crazy pilgrims. The snow was made more beautiful by the lack of wind. The snow that had fallen sat in the trees, an inch on the thinnest branches, and enhanced the white world around us. At the same time, of course, my shoes and socks, which I had meticulously dried the night before, were already wet as the slush seeped through my shoes.

We walked the rest of that day out of Portomarín, passing Spaniards on quiet country roads who were equally excited by the snow. Everyone seemed to have gone over to their neighbor's farm to stand outside and marvel. A Guardia Civil SUV had stopped outside a barn full of chickens to chat with the owner about the snow-covered roads. All of rural Galicia was outside — and rightly so — for the snow did not last long. As the temperature rose from the high 20's to the mid 30's, the snow began to disappear — first from the roads, then from the roofs, and finally from the trees.

Luckily, as we entered the hamlet of Eirexe, we saw a small bar which, surprisingly, looked open. From the cold and wet, we entered a place warm and dry. Bar stops in the winter are the most luxurious times of the day, and the snow made these even better. It is a wonderful feeling to take off your pack and wet jacket, and enjoy the heat of the room over a *café con leche*. In the winter, with so few customers, the bartenders are friendlier, wondering with interest why pilgrims hike in the winter. Even the food tastes better. The thick bread, large cuts of *lomo*, fried potatoes swimming in olive oil, and strong tannic wines of Galicia all fit a winter rather than a summer meal. The hospitality of the Camino, both historically in stories and in the present day, seems more relevant given the weather.

On one of our last nights on the Camino, we stayed in Olveiroa with two middle-aged Germans we had been hiking with for the past several days. It had rained off and on all afternoon, and as the sun began to set, the rain increased. While the rest of us hung up our wet clothes and stuffed newspaper in our shoes, my mother went to the *hospitalera* in the adjoining building to get dinner recommendations. Not a busy town even in the summer, the entire village had been driven behind closed doors by the rain and cold, and the streets were deserted. Not surprisingly, the only bar in town was closed for the day, so we were left with two options: piece together a meal from the store down the street, or ask the local bed and breakfast, closed for the winter, if they would open their doors to four wet pilgrims.

In the rain we walked down several blocks and knocked on the door. A middle-aged man answered, and we explained our predicament. I am unsure even today whether he was joking or serious, but he first said no, and then told us to return at 8 p.m., and he would start dinner. An hour later, dripping wet, we entered his house and were ushered into a small dining area next to an enormous fireplace, which was so large that two older men sat *inside* the fireplace, a small table between them, as they played cards. We were first brought bread and a rich *caldo gallego*, multiple bottles of wine, and pitchers of water. The next course was a huge pile of clams, steamed and then smothered in a rich orange sauce. Knowing that a Spanish meal cannot be complete without French fries, we were then served an enormous cut of *lomo* with fries, then a cheesecake made with cheese from the village cows. Amid the rich, authentic food and the buzz from the wine, we joked and told stories with the two Germans as if we had been good friends for years, knowing that tomorrow, as they headed to Finisterre and we headed to Muxia, we would never see them again. Perhaps the long, dreary, rainy day biased me in favor of the fare, but this was the tastiest and most enjoyable meal I have ever had. After we settled our bill (ten euros each — we usually paid more for worse food), the four of us scurried back in the rain to our *albergue*, and I quickly fell into a deep sleep.

Walking the Camino in winter presents its challenges — less daylight for walking, more *albergues* and bars are closed, few pilgrims — and the weather is often unpleasant. But these very experiences also allow the true essence of both Spain and the Camino to reveal itself: a barman opening because he sees a few pilgrims who need a *café con leche*; pilgrims realizing that a *hospitalera* has waited at the *albergue* all afternoon essentially for them; a local farmer querying why pilgrims choose to hike in the winter. The small villages of northern Spain offer something that few travelers see, but it is well worth walking through small stone-walled farms, to glimpse carefully tended vegetable gardens, fat cows, and the multitude of *hórreos* that represent a traditional method of farming and town organization that is in a very real sense dying out. Young Spaniards live in Santiago or León, not Negreira or Palas de Rei. To see these places in winter is to see them at their finest, when the Camino is no longer a freeway but a true walking trail. As we hiked past their farms, old Spaniards would come out and talk to us about the weather, often mixing *Gallego* and Spanish, as if we lived in their village. In this sense, walking in winter is the closest a pilgrim can come to the thousand-year-old idea of a pilgrimage.

ACKNOWLEDGMENTS

We owe a large debt of gratitude to George Greenia at the College of William & Mary for his encouragement of this project, which began as a presentation entitled "Younger Voices on the Camino" at the Seventh Annual Gathering of the American Pilgrims on the Camino in Williamsburg, Virginia. We thank him for permission to reprint Daniel W. Hieber's "18 Going on 19" which appeared in *American Pilgrim Magazine*, Vol. 1, No. 2 (Fall 2005).

We thank Roanoke College for its support of this project through a sabbatical leave for Lynn in Spring 2010 and for publication assistance. Lynn's colleagues at Roanoke College, who have long listened appreciatively and critically to her reflections on the Camino, have enhanced the development of this book. David Mulford generously created the book's graphics.

We also thank Michael Squires, to whom the book is dedicated. His unfailing support has always strengthened us both as we walked the Camino and as we developed this project. His excellent editorial advice has guided us in all phases of our work.

And, finally, we thank those who have walked the Camino with us, sharing conversation and meals, helping in time of need, and enlarging our understanding of pilgrimage: Florinda Ruiz, Roanoke College May Term students, Francisco Rodríguez Alvarez, Asunción Melero Donato, Ann Akers Hlusko, Beverly Prager, Geno Iannacone, Ben Shelton, Kate Carroll, the J2A group of Christ Episcopal Church (Blacksburg, Virginia), Linda Elliott Ambrose, Charlene Kalinoski, Sallie Smyth, Hans Striker, Dot McKewen, Cullen Hedlesky, and the many others whom we met along the way, but whose names we never knew. All of you touched us and enlivened our journeys. Truly the community of pilgrims makes the Camino a transformative experience.

FURTHER READING

SCHOLARLY STUDIES

Cousineau, Phil. *The Art of Pilgrimage: The Seeker's Guide to Making Travel Sacred.* Berkeley: Conari, 1998.

Frey, Nancy Louise. *Pilgrim Stories: On and Off the Road to Santiago.* Berkeley: U of California P, 1998.

Gitlitz, David M., and Linda Kay Davidson. *The Pilgrimage Road to Santiago.* New York: St. Martin's, 2000.

Melczer, William. *The Pilgrim's Guide to Santiago de Compostela.* New York: Italica, 1993.

Starkie, Walter. *The Road to Santiago.* London: John Murray, 1957.

Stokstad, Marilyn. *Santiago de Compostela in the Age of the Great Pilgrimages.* Norman: U of Oklahoma P, 1978.

PERSONAL NARRATIVES

Boers, Arthur Paul. *The Way is Made by Walking: A Pilgrimage Along the Camino de Santiago.* Downers Grove, IL: InterVarsity, 2007.

Chimenti, Wayne. *El Camino de Santiago: Rites of Passage.* Victoria, BC: Trafford, 2005.

Christmas, Jane. *What the Psychic Told the Pilgrim.* Vancouver, BC: Greystone, 2007.

Dennet, Laurie. *A Hug for the Apostle.* Toronto: Macmillan of Canada, 1987.

Egan, Kerry. *Fumbling: A Pilgrimage Tale of Love, Grief, and Spiritual Renewal on the Camino de Santiago.* New York: Doubleday, 2004.

Feinberg, Ellen. *Following the Milky Way: A Pilgrimage on the Camino de Santiago.* Ames: Iowa State UP, 1989. Second edition: Elyn Aviva, *Following the Milky Way: A Pilgrimage on the Camino de Santiago.* Boulder, CO: Pilgrims' Process, 2001.

Hitt, Jack. *Off the Road: A Modern-Day Walk Down the Pilgrim's Road Into Spain.* New York: Simon & Schuster, 1994.

Kerkeling, Hape. *I'm Off Then: Losing and Finding Myself on the Camino de Santiago.* Trans. Shelley Frisch. New York: Free Press, 2006.

Moore, Tim. *Travels with My Donkey: One Man and His Ass on a Pilgrimage to Santiago.* New York: St. Martin's Press, 2005.

Neillands, Rob. *The Road to Compostela.* Derbyshire, UK: Moorland, 1985.

Nimmo, Ben. *Pilgrim Snail: Busking to Santiago.* London: Flamingo, 2001.

Rupp, Joyce. *Walk in a Relaxed Manner: Life Lessons from the Camino.* Maryknoll, NY: Orbis, 2005.

Schell, Donald, and Maria Schell. *My Father, My Daughter: Pilgrims on the Road to Santiago.* New York: Church, 2001.

Thatcher, Guy. *A Journey of Days: Relearning Life's Lessons on the Camino de Santiago.* Renfrew, Ontario: General Store, 2008.

Wallis, Mary Victoria. *Among the Pilgrims: Journeys to Santiago de Compostela.* Victoria, BC: Trafford, 2003.

CONTRIBUTORS

Michael Burriss is currently a third-year doctoral student in 20th- and 21st-Century Peninsular Literature at the University of Georgia. He received an M.A. in Spanish from Auburn University in 2008 and a B.A. from Erskine College in 2006. He walked the Camino Francés in winter 2003 and the Camino de San Salvador and the Camino Primitivo in summer 2009. He also completed *hospitalero* training in Grañón in 2005. He has studied abroad extensively, including a year in Madrid, and has traveled through much of Mexico and Central America. He also lived in Taormina, Sicily, for a summer.

Drew A. Cumings-Peterson is originally from Ankeny, Iowa, but has lived in Iowa City for the last seven years. For his undergraduate studies, he attended the University of Iowa, where he majored in English and Spanish. He then attended the University of Iowa College of Law and will graduate in May 2011. His most time-consuming activity has been working on the *Iowa Law Review*, where he is Editor in Chief. Outside the university, he enjoys hiking, playing guitar, and reading Irish and Latin American poetry. He started walking the Camino Francés in June 2006 at St. Jean Pied de Port. Drew has recently married and plans to walk the Camino with his wife, Cassie, in the near future.

Megan Drohan, a native of Wheaton, Illinois, walked the Camino Francés in May 2008, beginning in León. Her trip to Spain in 2008 was her first experience traveling outside the United States. She has since studied abroad in France, visited other European nations, and interned for the Commission on Security and Cooperation in Europe (U.S. Helsinki Commission) in Washington, D.C. Megan is currently completing her final year at Roanoke College as a French, Spanish, and International Relations major. She was recently inducted into Phi Beta Kappa. Upon completion of her degree, Megan plans a career in international politics/foreign relations.

Deborah Gitlitz, a native Hoosier, now lives in Portland, Oregon, where the spectacular scenery almost compensates for the absence of fireflies and lightning storms. She works as a youth librarian and spends as much time as possible hiking, growing vegetables, volunteering as an environmental educator, and singing with friends. She also makes a lot of soup. Deborah walked the Camino Aragonés and Francés in 1987, beginning in Urdos, France.

Allison Gray is a Roanoke College graduate from northern Virginia, who has walked the Camino Francés twice, once in May 2001 (with Roanoke College) and again in May 2005, both times starting in Roncesvalles. After returning from her second trip, Allison began pursuing new dreams and became a licensed teacher. She currently teaches Spanish in Roanoke, Virginia. While she has no timeline for a return trip to Spain, she has high hopes that her second trip will not have been her last.

Daniel W. Hieber is a linguist who works with speakers of endangered languages to document and revitalize their languages. A graduate of the College of William & Mary (2008), with a degree in Linguistics and philosophy, Daniel currently works for the Rosetta Stone Endangered Language Program in his hometown of Harrisonburg, Virginia. In his spare time he teaches karate, plays piano, and studies fascinating things about languages. Daniel walked the Camino Francés from Roncesvalles in 2005 and 2006, and the Camino del Norte from San Sebastián in 2008.

Nicholas Hoekstra grew up in Comstock Park, Michigan, and attended the University of Michigan, graduating in 2006 with degrees in both Spanish and psychology. After graduation, Nick spent two years in Málaga, where he taught English and volunteered for the local association of the Camino de Santiago. He then spent two years teaching in the Japan Exchange and Teaching program in Kitakyushu. Nick practices Judo and Aikido on most days and tries to plan his life around his travels. He walked the Camino Francés in 2004 from León, and the Camino Portugués in 2007 from Tui.

Philip Jackson was born and raised in Spring, Texas, where he is a senior at Klein High School. When not hiking or in school, he can often be found using his computer or playing video games. He walked the Camino Francés with his grandfather in the summer of 2008 starting in Roncesvalles. Since then they have hiked together every summer, including a portion of the Colorado Trail in 2009 and several trails in San Antonio in 2010. Next year he hopes to attend Western State University in Gunnison, Colorado, where he will enjoy the many hiking options.

Ryan Jackson walked the Camino in 2008, hiking from Santander to Oviedo on the Camino del Norte, and then taking a bus to Astorga to finish walking to Santiago on the Camino Francés. A year later, he graduated from the College of William & Mary. He is now pursuing a Master of Divinity degree at Princeton Theological Seminary and resides in Plainsboro, New Jersey with his fiancée. Ryan plans to obtain a doctorate and spend his life teaching and taking students to walk the Camino. He enjoys philosophy, cooking, good Scotch, and long walks in Spain.

Tal Jacobs was born in Sumter, South Carolina. He went to Cannon School in Concord, North Carolina and currently attends Washington and Lee University. He walked the Camino Francés in the spring of 2009, starting in León. His experience inspired him to explore the world further, studying abroad in St. Andrews, Scotland, which is also a site of ancient pilgrimage and cultural heritage. He enjoys being a student and is particularly interested in biology and the natural world. He loves the outdoors and the spirituality it inspires.

Christian Man was born in Vienna, Austria, and grew up in Memphis, Tennessee. He holds a Bachelor's degree in Community Development from Covenant College and is currently managing an urban agricultural development project in south Memphis. He likes books, the wilderness, food, and metaphors. In March 2010, he and his friend, Douglas Williams, began the Camino Francés in Le Puy-en-Velay, France. They arrived in Santiago two-and-a-half months later.

Cory O'Brien is a first-class roustabout and professional vagabond. He has been known to write stories, perform raps about science and mythology, and juggle. He graduated from California State University, Los Angeles, at age 18, thanks to the University's Early Entrance Program, and has been traveling like a virus ever since. He walked the Camino Francés in December of 2009, starting in Pamplona and arriving in Santiago just in time for the New Year's celebrations. He is currently on a sort of cross-country misadventure in the good old U.S. of A.

Paul Oliver hiked the Camino Francés from St. Jean Pied de Port to Santiago in the summer of 2006. Born in Indiana, Paul spent most of his upbringing in Michigan. He currently lives and works in Washington, D.C. where he provides IT training and support for the U. S. Agency for International Development. He is an avid traveler, runner, and cyclist, and dreams of hiking the Camino again. Paul is a 2009 graduate of the University of Michigan.

Tim Price-O'Brien walked the Camino Francés in May 2008 as a Roanoke College student. His journey began in the town of León and continued 180 kilometers to Santiago. Now a college graduate with honors in Spanish, Tim hails from southwestern Virginia, where he lives with his family and many animals. Currently he is embarking on a year of volunteer service to AmeriCorps.

Jessica Hickam Roffe was born and raised in Galax, Virginia. She attended Roanoke College and received her bachelor's degree in Business Administration in 2003. She walked the Camino in May 2001, starting in Roncesvalles. After graduating, she returned to Spain for three months to study at the Estudio Sampere language institute in Alicante. After spending five years in San Diego, California she now lives with her husband, Peter, in New York City and works for Victoria's Secret Beauty. Since completing the Camino, she continues to pursue other challenges including walking on the Great Wall of China, scuba diving in the Great Barrier Reef, white water rafting in Yosemite, throwing tomatoes at La Tomatina, swimming with sharks and sting rays in Bora Bora, and skydiving over San Diego.

Andrew Talbot Squires is a senior at the College of William & Mary, majoring in English and government. After graduation, he plans to teach English in northern Spain for a year before applying to law school. He first walked the Camino Francés in 2004, starting in Roncesvalles, and has returned three times, walking the Camino Francés in 2006 and 2010 and the Camino Portugués in 2009. His hobbies include backpacking and canoeing.

Lynn K. Talbot is Professor of Spanish at Roanoke College in Salem, Virginia. She first walked the Camino in 1974, starting in St. Jean Pied de Port, and has returned a number of times, walking with students, her son, her friends, and alone. She lives in Blacksburg, Virginia, with her husband, Michael Squires, and their son Andrew. With her husband, she co-authored *Living at the Edge: A Biography of D. H. Lawrence and Frieda von Richthofen* and has published numerous articles on the Lawrences and contemporary Spanish narrative. In her free time, she enjoys traveling, reading, and gardening.

Anne Tolene is from Lincoln, Alabama, and attends the University of Alabama at Birmingham, majoring in international studies and foreign language. She is a member of the Experiential Learning Scholars Program and works as a Resident Assistant and an Outdoor Pursuits Trip Leader. She walked the Camino Francés in May and June 2010, starting from Roncesvalles.

Mallory Trowbridge grew up in Williamsburg, Virginia. She graduated from Roanoke College in May 2009 with a bachelor's degree in Spanish and a minor in elementary education. She walked the Camino Francés from León in 2008 as a part of a May Term course. Following graduation she returned to Spain and worked as an Au Pair. She now resides in Northern Virginia and is a high school Spanish teacher in Prince William County.

Ashleigh Volland Whitmore lives in Beaufort, not far from her hometown of Charleston, South Carolina, with her husband Matt and their cat Buddy. She is the Event Director at a country club outside of Hilton Head Island, conducting weddings and celebrations, and uses her Spanish often with co-workers and at *quinceañera* parties. She loves to garden and entertain in her home, and talks about her adventure on the Camino anytime the topic of life-changing experiences or memorable trips abroad comes up. She walked the Camino Francés in 2004, starting in Burgos, and is sure to return to the Camino, hoping to finish the entire journey from St. Jean Pied de Port. To quote from the last entry in her journal, "a piece of my heart most definitely remains in Spain."

Dave Whitson, from Seattle, Washington, is a pilgrimage addict. He has tried the 12-step program, but always seems to follow those with another 100,000 or so. He first walked the Camino Francés in May 2003, starting in St. Jean Pied de Port. Since then, he has been fortunate to not only revisit the Francés multiple times, but also the Caminos Aragonés, Primitivo, and Norte, Italy's Via Francigena, Norway's St. Olav's Way, and England's Canterbury Trail. He has also led six groups of high school students on pilgrimage, four in Spain and two in Italy. When not on pilgrimage, he is a high school history and literature teacher, a compulsive reader, and co-leader of the Legacy Project, which explores the legacy of violence and process of national transformation in countries recently scarred by war, rebellion, or oppression. You can find out more about Dave at www.walkingthroughtime.com.

CPSIA information can be obtained at www.ICGtesting.com
Printed in the USA
LVOW041248241112

308655LV00001B/120/P